HIGHER

SUCCESS WITH BEC

Published by:
Summertown Publishing Ltd
32–38 Saffron Hill
London EC1N 8FH

www.mcelt.co.uk

ISBN 978 1 902741 88 8

First published 2008
Reprinted 2009

Page design and setting: Oxford Designers & Illustrators
Illustrated by Clive Goddard pages 13, 32, 52, 60, 66, 67, 81, 90, 103, 119.
Cover design by white space
Cover image: Getty Images

Printed by Megaprint, Turkey

Acknowledgements
The author would like to thank David Riley for 'making a proper writer of me'.

The publishers would like to dedicate the Success with BEC series to the memory of its inspirational editor, David Riley.

The publishers would like to thank and acknowledge the following sources for diagrams, copyright material and trademarks:

Young workers want it all now, reproduced by permission of Associated Press.
Geneva fights prejudice with anonymous CVs, reproduced by permission of Swiss Info/Swiss radio International (SRI).
Job satisfaction, reproduced by permission of Simon Caulkin and The Observer.
I think like a wise man but communicate in the language of the people. W.B. Yeats, poet (1865-1939), permission granted by A P Watt Ltd on behalf of Gráinne Yeats.
Quotes from secrets of closing the sale by Zig Ziglar.
The ad revolution will not be televised, reproduced by permission of the author Owen Gibson.
World Stocks/Use - Palm Oil - graph used with the permission of HGCA.
How the supermarkets are squeezing their suppliers, reproduced by permission of The Financial Times.
Corporate universities, reproduced by permission of the author Matthias Becker.
Trading pollution quotas - from 'The Little Earth Book', reproduced with the permission of Alistair Sawday's.
Corporate Social Responsibility, reproduced by permission of Hubbards.
Icelands Energy Resources, reproduced by permission of the author Gwladys Fouche.
Getting Past No by William Ury, published by Random House Business Books. Reprinted by permission of The Random House Group Ltd.
Successful cross-cultural communication, reproduced from www.schulersolutions.com. Dr A.J. Schuler is an expert in leadership and organizational change. To find out more about his programs and services, visit www.SchulerSolutions.com or call (703) 370 6545.
The New Philanthropists, reproduced by permission of the author Simon Jenkins.

Summertown Publishing would also like to acknowledge the Business English Certificates Handbook (published by University of Cambridge ESOL Examinations) as the source of exam formats and rubrics in the Exam Spotlight lessons and other exam-type activities throughout the book.

Every effort has been made to trace and contact copyright holders prior to publication, in some cases this has not been possible. We will be pleased to rectify any errors or omissions at the earliest opportunity.

Photography
Getty Images pages 6, 7, 8, 11, 12, 23, 27, 28, 30, 31, 33. Baker Publishing Group page 36. Getty Images page 36. PA Photos page 39. Getty Images pages 41, 46. PA Photos page 47. Getty Images pages 49, 53, 57, 58, 61, 62, 63, 68, 73. PA Photos page 76 (Kermit the Frog), (hurricane). Getty Images page 76 (smog), (drought), (factory explosion). Penguin Co. UK page 78. Getty Images page 82. PA Photos page 86 (i-pod). Getty Images page 86 (dairy produce), (old fashioned telephone), (spanner). PA Photos page 88 (Model T Ford). Getty Images page 88 (mobile phone), (memory stick), (lightbulb). Random House page 92. Getty Images page 96. PA Photos page 97, 99. Getty Images page 101. PA Photos page 106, 107. Superstock (Lake Apoyo) page 110. Getty Images pages 110, 111, 113, 116, 118, 120, 122, 123.
Commissioned photography: Mark Mason pages 25, 104, 114.

Summertown Publishing would like to thank the following for their contribution in reviewing Success with BEC in its early stage of production:
Tessa Osborne, IFAGE Paroles, Switzerland
Alwena Sullivan, The Canterbury School of English, IFAGE, Switzerland
Amy Jost, International Companies, Switzerland
Barbara Heck, Fachhochschule, Nordwestschweiz, Switzerland
Caroline Häring, NSH Bildungszentrum, Switzerland
Celeste Zappolo Berger, EB Zurich, Migros, Switzerland
Elizabeth Delbreil, International Companies, Switzerland
Dr Holi Schauber, University of Fribourg, Switzerland
James Stauffer, EasyEnglish, KPMG, PWC, MSJC, Switzerland
Jayne Herzog, Klubschule, Migros, Switzerland
Lilli-Marie Pavka, Zurich Business School (KV), Switzerland
Norelee Wolf, Interlangues, Switzerland
Reto Hähni, Flying Teachers, Switzerland
Rosemarie Allemann, University of Applied Sciences, Switzerland
Rudolf Weiler, KVZ Business School, Switzerland
Sally Beale, IFAGE, The Canterbury School of English
Sandy Egloff, PLSs, Switzerland
Dave Davies, Asia Pacific Education, Cambridge ESOL Centre, Canada
Louise Rankin, Communication Skills Consultancy, Norway
Michael Williams, Fachhochschule Vorarlberg, Austria
Otto Weihs, University of Applied Sciences, Austria
James Schofield, Siemens, Germany

HIGHER

SUCCESS WITH BEC

THE NEW BUSINESS ENGLISH CERTIFICATES COURSE

STUDENT'S BOOK

PAUL DUMMETT with COLIN BENN

CONTENTS

1.1 Working life

VOCABULARY

Describing working life

1 What does this quotation mean to you?

'Life is what happens to you while you're busy making other plans.'
John Lennon, English singer & songwriter (1940–1980)

2 Discuss these questions.

1 How many jobs do you expect to have in your life? 1–3 4–7 8 or more
2 Would you prefer to be self-employed or an employee? Why?
3 In fifteen years' time, do you expect to be working more or less than now?
4 At what age do you expect to stop working? 55 65 75

3 Underline the best word to complete each sentence.

1 At the moment, people generally *retire / resign* at 65.
2 I *joined / applied for* the company when I was 25 and have worked there ever since.
3 What's the best way to *pay / reward* our employees for good performance?
4 About 700 staff were *laid off / dismissed* when the company lost the contract to supply Toyota.
5 We have *educated / trained* our staff in the use of laser equipment.
6 I'm going to *leave / change* the company at the end of the year.
7 E and G Consultants *recruits / employs* from the top business schools.
8 Companies need to offer parents of young children more *flexible / overtime* hours.
9 They used only to offer permanent posts, but now most new contracts are *temporary / part-time* ones.
10 I have one *day off / holiday* a week to attend a course at college.

4 Make sentences with the words you *didn't* use in Exercise 3.

5 Make nouns from the following verbs.

Verb	Noun	Verb	Noun
1 employ	employment	6 recruit	
2 promote		7 apply	
3 retire		8 dismiss	
4 resign		9 pay	
5 train		10 reward	

READING

Attitudes to work

6 **Do you think that people starting work now have a different attitude to work than their parents did? If so, in what ways?**

7 **Look at the newspaper article and read the title. What does the title suggest to you? Read the article and check if you were right.**

Young workers want it all, now

Oh, and they'll need to take next Friday off, too

DETROIT – Kurt Jennings, hoping to start a career in radio sales, thought he was prepared to answer any question during his recent interview. Then the radio executive opened the interview with, 'So, we call you guys the "Entitlement Generation". You imagine you're entitled to everything.'

There is an impression that the current generation of young workers has high expectations for salary, responsibility and job flexibility, but little appetite for hard work and little sense of loyalty to a company.

'A lot of twenty-somethings have a hard time making the transition to work – typically kids who've had success early in life and who've become used to getting instant gratification,' says Dr. Levi Cohen, a paediatrics professor. He says that coddling parents and colleges often fail to prepare students for the realities of adulthood and working life.

Many employers, from corporate executives to restaurateurs, agree.

'It seems they expect to have in their first week everything that the veteran has worked 20 or 30 years to earn,' says Mike Amor, the owner of a Salt Lake City chain of restaurants.

Kurt had this reply for his interviewer at the radio station: 'Maybe we were spoiled by your generation. But "entitled" is too strong a word,' he said. 'Do we think we're deserving if we're going to go out there and break our backs for you? Yes.'

He ended up getting the job.

But some experts say that having high expectations, and telling your boss what they are, isn't necessarily a bad thing.

'It's true they're not all rushing to bury themselves in a cubicle and follow orders for the next 40 years, but why on earth should they?' asks Jeff Bartlett, a University of Carolina psychologist.

8 **Do you think the younger generation is spoiled and expects too much? Or do you think the older generation sacrificed their lives (and fun in their lives) for work?**

9 **What do the following phrases from the text mean?**

1 little appetite for hard work
2 twenty-somethings
3 instant gratification
4 coddling parents and colleges
5 we were spoiled by your generation
6 break our backs for you
7 bury themselves in a cubicle

GRAMMAR

Grammar Tip

We say:
I am good at making decisions
but
He intends to run for President.

Gerund and infinitive

1 Which of the verbs or phrases in the box take the gerund (*-ing*) and which ones take *to* + infinitive (*to do*)?

~~be good at~~ ~~plan / intend / aim~~ be worth fail be reluctant have trouble / difficulty hope / expect manage succeed in decide think about / consider enjoy avoid involve have be used to / accustomed to be willing / prepared

+ gerund (*-ing*)	+ *to* + infinitive (*to do*)
be good at	*plan / intend / aim*
______	______
______	______
______	______
______	______
______	______
______	______
______	______
______	______

2 Which of the following pairs of phrases is the odd one out grammatically? Why?

1 be good at – be bad at
2 be willing – be reluctant
3 succeed in – fail
4 enjoy – dislike

3 Complete these sentences.

0 *When I retire, I plan to do some voluntary work for a charity.*
1 When I retire, I plan ...
2 I think I'm quite good at ...
3 Before attending a job interview, it's worth ...
4 My job involves ...
5 When speaking English, I often have difficulty ...
6 At work I feel satisfied if I manage ...
7 For my summer holiday this year, I am considering ...
8 If I was offered more money, I would be willing ...
9 The hardest thing about starting a new job is getting used to ...
10 I get annoyed with colleagues if they fail ...

4 Choose five of the phrases in exercise 1 and make sentences about your own working life.

LISTENING

Exam Success

Study the options carefully before listening. When listening, be aware that each correct answer on the page will paraphrase what you hear, ie have the same meaning, but use different words.

The future of human resources

5 1.1 **You will hear five human resources (HR) managers talking about the key issues in human resources facing companies today.**

- The first time you listen, indicate which employee group in the workforce they are talking about.
- The second time you listen indicate what actions they propose to take to deal with each issue.

TASK ONE – EMPLOYEE GROUP

1 ________

2 ________

3 ________

4 ________

5 ________

A older employees (50–60)
B new recruits
C trainees
D senior management
E young highly qualified employees
F women
G retired employees
H disabled workers

TASK TWO – PROPOSED ACTION

6 ________

7 ________

8 ________

9 ________

10 ________

A efforts to retain good employees
B the introduction of more flexible working arrangements
C linking salaries more closely to results
D more focus on job training for employees
E encouraging people back from retirement
F more support for working parents
G developing a more positive attitude towards older workers
H reducing staff costs

6 You've heard the priorities of HR managers. What are your priorities for your working life? Consider the following:

- flexible hours
- working environment
- pay
- training
- career prospects
- retirement

VOCABULARY

CVs and personal summaries

1 What do you call someone who ...?

0 employs people — *an employer*
1 is employed by a firm ________
2 applies for a job ________
3 is interviewed for a job ________
4 is seeking (looking for) a job ________
5 participates in something ________
6 has left university with a degree ________

2 Do this exercise from an online guide for employers.

Guide for employers

CVs and covering letters are essential tools in the search for the right candidate for the job and you should use them as a snapshot of a potential candidate. Being able to read between the lines will help you in your task of putting the right person in the right job.
Look at these three examples of *personal summaries* from first-time job applicants received by a leading consultancy firm. Which applicant would you employ and why?

1 A dynamic and knowledgeable IT graduate who can bring success to your business, I have excellent interpersonal skills and considerable experience of designing software solutions. Whether working as part of a team or independently, I have the ability to come up with the goods.

2 I am a successful business entrepreneur seeking to return to a large organisation after years of running my own company. I have experience of all aspects of business and would welcome the chance to share this expertise with clients of a forward-looking consultancy firm.

3 A self-motivated graduate with a masters in economics, I have pre-course experience in the Economic Studies department of a subsidiary of Exxon Mobil, where I enjoyed six months working with the back office team. Adaptable, efficient and keen to learn.

READING

The anonymous CV

3 Underline which elements should definitely be included in a CV (the others are 'optional extras').

1 name
2 address
3 telephone number
4 email address
5 age / date of birth
6 sex
7 marital status
8 nationality
9 personal summary
10 personal qualities
11 goals and objectives
12 education – primary, secondary, higher education
13 other skills or qualifications (membership of associations, driving licence, etc)
14 employment history – company, job title, responsibilities, results
15 hobbies and interests
16 languages
17 references
18 personal achievements

4 Read the first part of the text. What is the idea behind an anonymous CV?

Geneva fights prejudice with anonymous CVs

Prospective employees in Geneva are to send in anonymous job applications as part of a pilot project to tackle discrimination.

The trial, the first of its kind in Switzerland, has been launched by the canton's integration office and involves three major employers.

Retailer Migros, energy provider SIG and the commune of Vernier have all signed up to participate in the scheme.

Under the terms of the project, which will last for three months, job-seekers will send in CVs detailing their skills and experience but omitting their name, address, age, sex, any religion or disability and photo.

The aim is to give all applicants an equal chance of being called up for interview.

'It is impossible to quantify but we know there is much more discrimination than we are aware of. There are some unemployed people who are not getting interviews because they are of a different nationality, colour or religion,' André Castella, head of the project, told Swissinfo.

'The important thing is that candidates who have the right skills for a job should be seen, and we want to give them the chance to be heard. There are employers out there who refuse to consider Africans.'

5 Read the second part of the text and put one word in each space.

Castella said another aim of the trial was to encourage employers (**0**) *and* the public to talk about discrimination and to raise awareness about the scale of injustice.

He added that the idea of anonymous CVs had already been tested in France where the country's National Assembly is due to consider making the practice mandatory for all firms (**1**) ________ more than 50 employees.

Jean-Charles Bruttomesso, Director of Human Resources at Migros Geneva, said all applications for positions until June 30 (**2**) ________ be considered purely on the basis of skills and experience. He noted that the retailer's involvement in the project was part of ongoing equal opportunity efforts.

'This initiative is an occasion for (**3**) ________ of us to think about our prejudices and other preconceived ideas and question them,' he said.

Those behind the scheme admit that an anonymous CV will (**4**) ________ rule out the possibility of discrimination once a candidate arrives for an interview but they stress (**5**) ________ it is an important first step. The launch of the pilot project forms part of the canton's week-long series of events (**6**) ________ racism and discrimination.

6 Do you think this initiative will be effective in eliminating discrimination by employers?

1.2 Asking and answering questions

LISTENING

An environmental accident

The Daily Reporter

Tanker Grounded

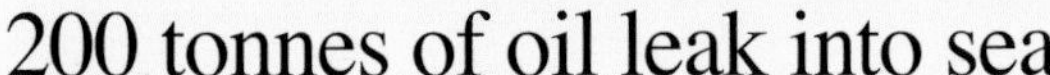
200 tonnes of oil leak into sea

1 1.2 **Following this news announcement, a journalist interviews a spokesperson from the company that owns the tanker. Listen to the interview.**

1 What caused the accident?
2 How many accidents has the ship been involved in?
3 Does the spokesperson come out of it well?

2 Complete the questions the journalist asks.

1 ____________________ how this happened?
2 This isn't the first time this particular ship has been in an accident, ____________________?
3 And ____________________ to do to limit the damage?
4 ____________________ this kind of accident is acceptable?
5 It's a PR disaster for your company, ____________________?

GRAMMAR

Indirect questions

3 Look at exercise 2. Study the structure of the indirect questions in sentences 1 and 4, and the tag questions in sentences 2 and 5.

4 Convert the following questions into indirect questions.

0 How many years' experience do you have in customer service?
Can you tell me how many years' experience you have in customer service?
1 Where have you worked before?
I'd be interested to know ____.
2 Are you an ambitious person?
Would you say ____?
3 Have you gone as far as you can in your present job?
Do you think ____?
4 Who are our main customers?
Do you know ____?

5 **Convert the following questions into tag questions.**

0 Are you interested in a full-time job?
You're interested in a full-time job, aren't you?

1 Are you married?
____?

2 Can't you start tomorrow?
____?

3 Have you only worked for smaller companies?
____?

4 Did you manage to find our offices easily?
____?

5 Is this your first real job?
____?

6 Would you be able to work part-time?
____?

SPEAKING

A job interview

6 **How would you feel if you were asked these questions? How would you reply?**

1 Can you tell me why you think you'll be good at this job?
2 Why should I employ you?
3 You don't have much experience in this field, do you?
4 You've taken quite a lot of time out from work. Why is that?
5 You are quite a quietly-spoken person. Do you have trouble asserting yourself?
6 Now, your last job. Did you choose to leave?
7 And what do you know about our company?
8 So tell me what you did yesterday.

7 **Work with a partner. Each choose one of the following jobs to be interviewed for. Prepare five questions each and then take it in turns to adopt the role of interviewer and interviewee. Try to put your interviewee 'on the spot'.**

firefighter restaurant manager web designer
fundraiser for local sports club trainee investment advisor

1.3

Reading Test: Introduction and Part One

EXAM FORMAT

The Reading Test has six parts, in which there are a total of 52 questions, and lasts one hour. It carries 25% of the total marks. The texts are all business-related and vary between 150 and 500 words in length. Each part tests a particular reading skill or understanding of language structure.

Exam Success

Intheexam,youhave an hour to read over 2,000 words, so try to develop your reading speed. The only way to do this is to practise:

- Read English business texts, eg *Time*, *Newsweek*.
- Getyournewsfrom English Internet sites, eg the BBC, CNN.

Part	Text type	Skill focus	Task
1	Single text or 5 short texts (450 words)	Reading for global meaning; summarising	Matching summaries to each section of text
2	Single text (450–500 words)	Reading for detail; understanding structure	Inserting missing sentences into text
3	Single text (500–600 words)	Reading for general meaning and specific detail	4-part multiple choice comprehension questions
4	Single text (250 words)	Understanding meaning and grammar of individual words	Gap-fill; multiple choice (4-choice)
5	Single text (250 words)	Finding missing words to give meaning and cohesion	Open gap-fill (one word per gap)
6	Single text (150–200 words)	Understanding grammatical structure	Identifying incorrect or unnecessary words

APPROACH

Part One

Part One is a test of reading for gist or global meaning. Five texts or sections have to be matched to five sentences that summarise the general view being expressed in each. Follow these steps.

- Read the instructions twice and make sure you understand the context of the passage(s) and what you are being asked to do.
- Do not read the summaries first.
- Bearing in mind what general information you are looking for, read the first text and then try to summarise, in your head, the general view it expresses.
- Now read the summaries and find the one that matches your own mental summary.
- Repeat this procedure for each of the other four texts.

KEY SKILL

Summarising

1 **Write a one-sentence summary for this passage. Compare your answer with your partner.**

I favour a direct approach to interviewing where the questions really put the candidate under pressure and test their reactions. If you look at manuals on interviewing technique, you'll find that most advise you first to make the candidate feel at ease, and then to ask open-ended questions that give them the freedom to talk and express themselves as they would like. But I think we're being far too nice here. By allowing people to dictate the direction of the interview, we run the risk of not discovering who they really are and wasting everyone's time.

EXAM PRACTICE

2 **Following the approach described above, do this Reading Test Part One. Give yourself about twelve minutes.**

PART ONE

Questions 1–8

- Look at the sentences below and at the five extracts from an article on employee motivation.
- Match each statement **1–8** to one of the extracts (**A, B, C, D** or **E**).
- You will need to use some of the letters more than once.
- There is an example at the beginning, (**0**).

Example:

0 Job satisfaction is the key to an employee's motivation. D

1 Companies usually try to motivate employees with extra payment or verbal praise.
2 Financial rewards don't work so well when the manager assesses performance himself.
3 In the end, motivation has to come from the person himself.
4 Loyalty and commitment are two different things.
5 Employees are committed when they understand and believe in the company's aims.
6 Most employees see rewards as an end in themselves.
7 How well you work does not depend on how good your working conditions are.
8 Good relations between managers and workers create the right working environment.

A

Fundamental to the issue of motivation is the distinction between employee loyalty to the company and employee commitment. Employees feel loyal when they feel comfortable and well looked after: job security, reasonable conditions of pay, generous holiday entitlement, medical insurance and a good pension. Without these conditions an employee will feel neither loyalty to the company nor any motivation to work. But it is also possible that even with good conditions, the employee may not feel motivated. This is because performance is not directly related to working conditions: an employee can feel secure, whether he works hard or not.

B

Motivation has more to do with commitment to the job. The conditions that produce commitment are different from those that inspire loyalty. Committed employees will have a clear sense of the goals of the company and understand their part in contributing to achieving them. Moreover, they will believe that these goals are worth working for: they will derive job satisfaction from what they do. So companies who want a motivated staff ought to be spending their time thinking about their goals and communicating these with enthusiasm to their staff.

C

Instead, the motivation debate seems to focus on rewards, either financial or non-financial. For example, money is commonly used as an incentive for sales people or others with measurable targets to reach. Sometimes it is also used to reward employees whose performance has been evaluated subjectively by a line manager. This is less satisfactory. Verbal commendation is also used to motivate, from a simple word of encouragement in the employee's ear to a public award ceremony.

D

But do all these types of rewards motivate people? Well, yes, they do. They motivate them to get rewards. What they don't necessarily do is motivate them to be a committed employee and do a good job. What really motivates people is the level of satisfaction they find in their work. As Herzberg famously put it: 'If you want people motivated to do a good job, give them a good job to do.'

E

So the real motivators are things which are intrinsic to the job: that the employee feels part of a unit that is working towards something worthwhile. And from this, as long as communication between employee and management is open and respectful, will come recognition for good work, advancement in the company and personal growth. The best that companies can do is to create such an environment and then hope that within it people are able to motivate themselves.

2.1 Growing the company

VOCABULARY

Parts of a company

1 Do you think this quotation is true for all businesses?

'I think that our fundamental belief is that for us growth is a way of life and we have to grow at all times.'

Mukesh Ambani, Chairman of Reliance Industries

2 Read this entry from a company website and use these words to label the diagram.

subsidiary headquarters sales offices
warehouses R&D division main plant

We are based in La Défense, the business district of Paris, and new products are developed nearby at our labs in St Denis. Our principal manufacturing facility is just outside Lille and products go from there to a central distribution point at Compiègne. Three sales agencies cover the various regions of France with international offices in Frankfurt, Milan and Madrid. The London office is run by our UK subsidiary.

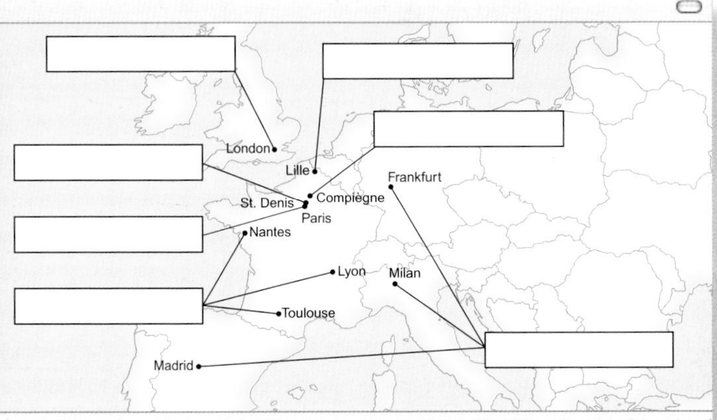

3 What is the difference between the following words and phrases?

1 a *sales office* and a *subsidiary*
2 a *warehouse* and a *plant*
3 the *headquarters* and a *division*

VOCABULARY

Growth strategy

4 Find a synonym in the box for each of the underlined words.

go public sell off set up go out of business expand
take over make redundant shut down

1 We acquired Everforce Ltd in 2005.
2 Our target is to grow the business by 15% each year.
3 We created a subsidiary to sell after-sales services.
4 The company will be listed on the Stock Exchange next year.
5 They went bankrupt last year.
6 We laid 300 employees off in June.
7 After a lot of discussion we decided to close the plant.
8 We have divested our shares in the logistics company.

5 What is the difference between the following expressions?

1 *laying* people *off* and *firing* them
2 *taking over* a company and *merging* with it
3 *organic growth* and *non-organic growth*

READING

6 **SAP and Oracle are the world's leading companies in providing software solutions for business. But their business strategies are very different.**

Read the text about SAP's growth strategy. Choose the best sentences from the list (A–H) below to complete each gap (1–6). Do not use any letter more than once.

SAP competes with 'organic growth'

How do you stay at the top of the heap in the business software game? If you're SAP, you do it through 'organic growth', not blockbuster acquisitions. That's the word from SAP CEO Henning Kagermann. (**0**) H.

'The second-best strategy is acquisition,' Kagermann said. 'The best is organic growth. We are not just doing organic growth because we have no other choices.'

The comment was aimed squarely at rival Oracle Corp., which spent nearly $20 billion between 2004 and 2006 expanding its core database business into the SAP-dominated business applications market. (**1**) ______. 'We are the market leader,' he said. 'It's no surprise that a distant number-two player wants to catch up.'

SAP was set up in 1972 by five former IBM employees. (**2**) ______. Although it has a growing number of subsidiaries, these are complements to its main activities, as Shai Agassi, president of the company's Product and Technology Group explained, at the same time having a direct dig at Oracle. The key difference between the two companies, he says, lies in Oracle's tendency to 'acquire an industry solution that is at the heart'. 'When we do an acquisition, it's at the edge of the solutions. (**3**) ______ Oracle is buying half body parts and trying to make a body out of it.'

In fact, Agassi expects SAP to grow faster than the rest of the industry this year – 15% to 17% in sales of new software licences – through internal innovation and small-scale acquisitions. (**4**) ______.

SAP used to concentrate on large business customers, but is increasingly pursuing sales in the midmarket, a strategy that began in 2000. (**5**) ______.

The company expects to finish development of the mySAP suite within the next four years, as well as its Enterprise Services Architecture (ESA). ESA is basically a platform that will allow SAP to provide consistent business services around it, in much the same way as Microsoft has built applications around its successful operating systems.

Among the company's other goals is the development of hundreds of additional services for the mySAP suite, a so-called 'ecosystem' of supportive technologies.

'Business in the future is not business in an enterprise,' Kagermann says. 'It's business in an ecosystem. (**6**) ______. We try to invite others with great ideas to innovate on the platform.'

Exam Success

Make sure that the phrase you choose fits grammatically and in meaning, both with the sentence before and the sentence after. Read the whole text back to yourself at the end.

A In fact, it expects sales to companies with fewer than 25,000 employees to account for nearly half SAP's total software sales this year.

B They recently announced they had purchased Virsa Systems, a privately held supplier of regulatory compliance software.

C You just can't do everything yourself if you want to remain competitive.

D Competition in the market is fierce and only the big players will survive.

E Since then, it has evolved from a small, regional enterprise into the global market leader in ERP software, employing more than 34,000 people.

F Kagermann was unimpressed with Oracle's appetite for big, headline-grabbing acquisitions (PeopleSoft, Siebel Systems).

G That is different from buying half of a heart.

H He made the comments while he was talking with reporters last week during his company's annual Developer Kickoff Meeting in Burlingame, CA.

7 **Summarise the growth strategies of SAP and Oracle. What is the key to SAP's longer-term strategy?**

GRAMMAR

Past tenses

1 Study these extracts from the text about SAP on page 17.

- Name each underlined tense (past simple, past continuous, past perfect, present perfect or *used to*).
- Say what you know about each tense's use and why you think it is used here.

1 He made the comments while he was talking with reporters last week.
2 SAP was set up in 1972 by five former IBM employees.
3 Since then, it has evolved from a small, regional enterprise into the global market leader.
4 They recently announced they had purchased Virsa Systems.
5 SAP used to concentrate on large business customers, but is increasingly pursuing sales in the midmarket.
6 It's a strategy that began in 2000.

2 You receive this internal email. Follow the instructions in it.

Hi Denise
Below is the short company history I've written for the 'About us' entry on the English page of the new website. I think it's generally OK but I'm so unconfident about my use of tenses in English that I've just left the verbs in the infinitive! Can you put them in the right form and send it back? Thanks and sorry for being so useless!
Brigitte

This is the unusual story of Raincoat Software, a company that **(1)** __________ (come) into being accidentally because of the hobby of one man, Hans Meier.

In 1998 Hans **(2)** __________ (work) as a computer programmer for a large bank in Zurich. But he **(3)** __________ (be) restless. Each evening he **(4)** __________ (return) home and, just for fun, **(5)** __________ (hack) into official websites on his personal computer (not the bank's, of course!). The day after he **(6)** __________ (hack) onto a particularly sensitive US government website, he **(7)** __________ (receive) an email from them. Fearing that this would be the end of his career as a hacker and at the bank, he **(8)** __________ (open) it. It **(9)** __________ (be) a request from the US government, asking if he **(10)** __________ (want) a job as a security advisor.

Rather than taking a job as a government employee, Hans Meier **(11)** __________ (see) the opportunity to make a successful business out of computer security protection. Raincoat Software **(12)** __________ (be) born.

Since then, the company **(13)** __________ (employ) over 50 'security experts' – in others words, people with a similar background to our founder. We **(14)** __________ (help) over 300 large companies and government departments and are now a $100 million a year business.

But did the US government think it **(15)** __________ (take) a risk by employing Hans Meier all those years ago? The answer they **(16)** __________ (give) then is still the company's motto today: 'Better safe than sorry'.

WRITING

Writing about the past

3 Write a short piece (100 words approx) about a turning point in your life, work or studies: a moment when you decided to pursue a different route from the one you had up to that point. Use the following questions to help you.

1 What were you doing before that?
2 What happened to change your life?
3 What happened next?

READING

Mergers and acquisitions

4 **What happens when companies merge or acquire other companies? Look at the table below and make notes.**

	Opportunities	Threats
Employees		
Shareholders		
Customers		
Suppliers		

5 **In December 2004 Oracle, the world's second largest business software applications provider, took over PeopleSoft, the third largest. Read the letter that the CEO of PeopleSoft, Dave Duffield, wrote to his employees.**

1 Does he think the takeover will benefit employees or not?
2 Which of these adjectives best describes his feelings about the takeover?
bitter / resigned / angry

This is a sad day for me, and I'm sure an equally sad day for you.

It is now clear that Oracle will acquire our company. Over the past few weeks, our independent directors met with individual stockholders to get their views. We were told during these conversations that they believed Oracle's $24 wasn't adequate and did not reflect PeopleSoft's real value. It became clear to us that the vast majority of our stockholders would accept $26.50 and Oracle was willing to pay for it.

You should know, and I hope you would expect, that I am deeply saddened by this outcome. We have come so far under such trying circumstances over the past eighteen months, and especially the past two and a half months. PeopleSoft had gained significant momentum in all areas of our company, including with customers, prospects, and in the financial community.

Over the next few weeks, we will be working with Oracle to ensure that you get answers to as many questions as possible that you have. I believe some of you will find interesting opportunities at Oracle, others will take your talents and work elsewhere in the area that you live, while another group may have difficulties finding rewarding job experiences. It is to this last group that I offer my sincerest apologies for not figuring out a different conclusion to our 18-month saga.

I know it is little comfort, but I am extraordinarily proud of what we have accomplished over the past 17-plus years, and longer in the case of JD Edwards. And I am even prouder of you for your perseverance and teamwork over the past eighteen months.

I make a final request. And that is to continue our work with our heads held high. Whether it's serving customers, building products or working on internal operations, PeopleSoft and the people at PeopleSoft have built their reputation as a company with class.

Sincerely,

Dave

LISTENING

The PeopleSoft takeover

1 2.1 **Listen to two accounts of the takeover by a commentator and an industry analyst, both close to the takeover. What are the main differences in the working environment and the way employees were rewarded at the two companies?**

2 2.1 **Listen again and answer the questions. For each question (1–6), mark one letter (A, B or C) for the correct answer.**

1 What is said about how consultants are deployed in big IT consulting companies?
A They are given jobs with a lot of responsibility.
B They are often expected to learn on the job.
C They only work on projects where they have proven experience.

2 What does the commentator say about salaries at PeopleSoft?
A At least the company was open about its pay policy.
B They were at the market rate for the job.
C They were unacceptably low.

3 How did employees feel about their CEO, Dave Duffield?
A That he respected them and looked after them.
B That he was ready to leave the company.
C That he developed good software applications.

4 What does the commentator imply happened after the merger?
A The company's reputation suffered.
B People grew to respect the new CEO.
C A lot of people lost their jobs.

5 How does the industry analyst defend the company's growth strategy?
A He says size is very important in this industry.
B If Oracle hadn't taken over PeopleSoft, someone else would have.
C He says it will make them the biggest company in the sector.

6 How does he explain the differences in company culture?
A The two CEOs had a different philosophy.
B The two companies were involved in different types of business.
C There was no real difference.

WRITING

A press release

3 **You work in the press office of an insurance company that has recently taken over another company. Since the take-over there have been some negative reports about it. You decide to put out a press release. Include the following points.**

- Explain the business reasons for the take-over (to compete with other big insurance companies; to rationalise staffing).
- Express your enthusiasm about the future opportunities for the merged company.
- Thank all the employees for their support.
- Reassure people that there won't be major job cuts.

Begin like this:

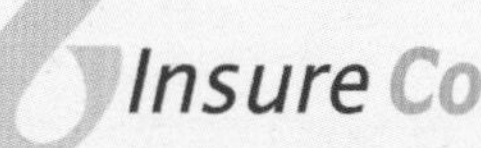

PRESS RELEASE

Last month Insure Co was pleased to announce the acquisition of ABC Insurance. The new company brings together two leading insurance providers to form the world's third largest insurance company ...

READING

4 **Read this extract from an article in *Business Strategy* magazine. Where do these four types of organisation belong in the text?**

stock brokers restaurants oil companies banks

Business Strategy **magazine, May**

Organisational culture

	Low risk	High risk
Rapid feedback and reward	Work-hard, play-hard culture	Tough-guy macho culture
Slow feedback and reward	Process culture	Bet-the-company culture

A lot of attempts have been made to categorise the organisation and culture of different companies, but only two things seem certain: 1) that many different cultures and types of organisation can exist within each company – and 2) that the activity and sector play a crucial role in determining how work is organised. Deal and Kennedy recognised this when they proposed four different types of organisational culture:

Work-hard, play-hard culture tends to apply to companies like software developers or (**1**) ______________ which need to react quickly to changing circumstances and to work at a high tempo. Creativity often plays an important part in their work so they tend to be organised in a project-based way, grouping people in teams to solve particular tasks.

Tough-guy macho culture concentrates power around key personnel, but it will also devolve a lot of responsibility to the individual and emphasise decisions that affect the present rather than the future. Examples are (**2**) ______________ sports teams, police, the military.

Process culture applies to companies which have strict hierarchies and strict job roles, such as insurance companies, (**3**) ______________ and public services. Strategy and direction seem to take second place to organisation and so they are often, maybe unfairly, associated with plodding and bureaucracy.

Bet-the-company culture may also be present in companies with a hierarchical structure, but long-term planning and investment, involving high risk, is also a key feature, so direction and goals are generally clearer. Examples are aircraft manufacturers and (**4**) ______________.

5 **Describe an organisation you know or have worked or studied in.**

1 How many people worked there?
2 What was its business / speciality?
3 How was it organised?
4 How would you describe the culture?

Did it fall into any of the categories described above? In what ways?

SPEAKING

An employee survey

6 **Look at this survey from the same edition of *Business Strategy* magazine. Mark the six items that are most important to you (1 is the most important).**

Business Strategy **magazine, May**

I prefer an organisation which emphasises:

A Individual responsibility and empowerment of employees
B Teamwork and consensus
C Clear lines of reporting and areas of responsibility
D Quick decision-taking and action
E Long-term, careful planning
F Creativity, innovation and taking risks
G Clear and consistent procedures
H Job security
I Customer satisfaction
J Measurable results
K Employee welfare
L Financial reward for employees
M Non-financial rewards (training, career development)
N Informal relationships between staff and management

7 **Discuss your answers with your partner. Taking into account his or her preferences, what job and type of company would you recommend?**

2.2 Presenting facts

LISTENING

Falling shares

1 **Read these two documents: a short article from a financial newspaper and a pre-Christmas advertisement from Kaptoys. What kind of company is it? What's the problem for Kaptoys?**

Shares in Kaptoys fell again today by 2% prompting speculation that the company will post poor profits for the second quarter running. The fall would be in line with other high street retailers who have all reported quieter sales than normal for the period.

2 2.2 **Listen to the short speech by Sheila Kaplan, CEO of Kaptoys, to her Business Development department. Complete the notes on her instructions.**

Meeting with:	*Sheila Kaplan*
Date:	*Thursday 17 April*
Progress with 3-year plan:	(1) ______
Consequences:	(2) ______
Action proposed:	(3) ______
Details to note:	(4) ______

SPEAKING

Presenting facts

3 **After a month's research the Business Development team meet again to present their findings. Work with a partner. You are each going to prepare a presentation.**

- Student A, look at the notes on the company on page 23 and prepare to present it.
- Student B, look at the notes on the company on page 127 and prepare to present it.
- Before you make your presentation, look first at the language box below. Use any phrases that you find useful. Remember that you are just presenting facts and not trying to sell something.

Presenting facts

OK. If everyone is ready, I'll begin. / Shall we begin? / Shall we get started?
I'm going to describe / present / explain / give you some information about ...
Please interrupt me if there's something that's not clear.
Please leave your questions until the end and I'll answer them then.
I'd like to begin by (saying / describing / explaining) ...
There are two / three / four key points to note about ...
Firstly ... Secondly ... And finally ...
It's also worth noting that ...
So, I think I've covered the main points.
So, to sum up, ...
I'd like to invite your questions now. / So, are there any questions?
So, (if there aren't any more questions) I'll end there. Thanks for your attention.

Student A

Company name:	Wheels Times 2
Company type:	Limited company, equal shares owned by two directors
Date established:	1989
Turnover:	£24 million per year
Number of employees:	65
Main products:	Children's and adults' bicycles; cycling accessories; cycling holidays
Locations:	Sixteen retail outlets in major cities across the UK; good Internet presence, with growing on-line sales

Brief history:

1989 – two mountain bike enthusiasts open shop in Manchester
1992 – voted best bike shop in UK by *Mountain Bike* magazine
1994 – three new shops in London, Cardiff and Birmingham
1998 – extends range, five new shops
2000 – offers cycling weekends and holidays
2001 – launches online bike shop
2004 – online sales hit £1m mark
2006 – seven new shops

Core competencies:	Technical knowledge of bicycles; customer service
Financial situation:	Positive cashflow; good profit margins; quite high debt from recent investment in new shop premises
Market prospects:	Good. Cycling increasingly popular and bikes increasingly sophisticated
Market price:	Probably high

4 **Discuss which of the two companies would be a better acquisition target for Kaptoys.**

2.3 Speaking Test: Introduction and Part One

EXAM FORMAT

The Speaking Test has three parts and lasts about fourteen minutes. For this part of the test you will be with at least one other candidate (and sometimes two). It carries 25% of the total marks. Each part tests a different speaking skill.

Part	Speaking task	Grouping	Length
1	Talking about yourself and expressing opinions	One-to-one	About 3 minutes
2	One-minute presentation on a business theme (choice of three) followed by questions from other candidates	Individual and pairwork	About 6 minutes
3	Discussion of a business scenario from prompts	Pairwork	About 5 minutes

Exam Success

Fourteen minutes goes very quickly. Make sure you use every opportunity to take the floor and interact with the other candidate and the examiner, while respecting their right to do the same.

Part 1: tests your ability to have a conversation about yourself (past, present and future) and to give opinions on general topics.
Part 2: tests your ability to organise, present and discuss information and ideas.
Part 3: tests your ability to interact in a business context, using appropriate functional language (agreeing, making suggestions, justifying, etc).

APPROACH

Part One

Part One should be a relaxed conversation. You can prepare by thinking about what to say about your studies, work, ambitions, interests and where you live. You can also learn idiomatic phrases for giving opinions, agreeing and disagreeing, etc.

KEY SKILL 1

Talking about yourself and your work

1 These are questions the examiner might ask you in the first part of the Speaking Test. Match each question (1–8) with one of the answers (A–H) below.

1 What do you like doing in your spare time? H
2 What do think of ... as a place to live?
3 What are you planning to do after the course?
4 What kind of course is it?
5 How would you describe your working environment?
6 Tell me a bit about the company.
7 What is your role exactly?
8 How would you feel about working until you're 70?

A We provide ... services to the ... industry.
B I'm going to apply for a job with ...
C It's a four-year degree course.
D I like it, but I miss my home town.
E It's quite relaxed / informal / traditional / dynamic.
F I work as a junior manager / a trainee.
G I'm not really sure it's necessary.
H My main interests are keeping fit and travelling.

KEY SKILL 2

Expressing opinions

2 **Discuss the points below with your partner. Use the phrases on page 130 to help.**

- Do you think it's better to work for a big organisation or a small company?
- Can management of people be learned, or is it a natural quality?
- What do you think will be the really big growth areas of the economy over the next fifteen years?

EXAM PRACTICE

3 **Use these examiner's prompts to simulate Part One of the test. Work with a partner and take it in turns to play the roles of examiner and candidate.**

Interview 1

After general introductions, ask the candidate about where they live, focusing on:

- the main industries of the town
- employment opportunities
- their opinion of the transport infrastructure
- if they would prefer to live somewhere else

Interview 2

After general introductions, ask the candidate about where they want to work in the future focusing on:

- skills and training needed for the job
- career prospects
- rewards of the job (financial and non-financial)
- their opinion of the prospects for this sector

3.1 Communication at work

VOCABULARY

Means of communication

1 What does this quotation mean to you?

'Think like a wise man but communicate in the language of the people.'
W.B. Yeats, poet (1865–1939)

2 Delete the verb that does NOT go with each type of business communication.

0 an email	send / draft / ~~post~~
1 a phone call	do / make / receive
2 a press release	put up / issue / put out
3 an advertising campaign	launch / run / make
4 a presentation	give / make / tell
5 a meeting or seminar	hold / attend / carry out
6 a report	produce / run / publish
7 a notice	put out / put up / display
8 a memo to all concerned	publish / send out / circulate
9 information on the Internet	post / make / put

3 For which of the following would you feel most confident using your English? And least confident? Discuss with your partner.

a presentation   a meeting   a phone call   a report   an email

READING

4 Discuss these questions with your partner.

1 Have you had good experiences of dealing with companies through call centres?
2 Do you shop on the Internet? Why? / Why not?
3 With which products or services is face-to-face contact helpful? With which is it unnecessary?

5 Read the five extracts from the magazine *Management Now* on page 27 and then match each of the eight statements (1–8) with one of the extracts. You will need to use some of the texts more than once.

0 You can gather a lot of customer data with modern computer systems. A
1 One future trend will be more direct contact between companies and their customers. _____
2 Business hasn't really changed, only the media of communication. _____
3 Companies need to think about which channel is most appropriate to their customers' needs. _____
4 Customers are frequently frustrated by not being put through quickly to the person they need to speak to. _____
5 There is less human interaction nowadays, but this isn't necessarily bad for the customer. _____
6 Companies can make economies by replacing people with machines and new technologies. _____
7 Rather than make contact easier some communication channels make contact more difficult. _____
8 The IT system failed to deliver the results the company wanted. _____

Better communication?

'THE MORE ELABORATE OUR MEANS of communication, the less we communicate.' These were the words of Joseph Priestly over 200 years ago. But if that was true then, what would he make of communications technology today? Natalie Fitzgerald asked five people working in the field what they thought.

A **Bill Osmond, data analyst**
I think he's got a good point. Powerful IT systems give companies enormous amounts of information on customer behaviour, but it's what they can do with this data that matters. A good example in recent years was Centrica, the British utility company. It acquired a big portfolio of different companies and then spent huge amounts of money on an IT system designed to cross-sell its various products and services – financial services, telephone contracts, energy supply and so on – to the customers in its different businesses. But they never managed to do it, because their IT people were unable to merge all the customer databases or to make them talk to each other.

B **Sarah Bridgestone, former call centre manager**
Absolutely. Call centres can more often act as a barrier than a help. Take the example of a well-known mobile phone operator. When a customer calls, he's given a list of options to choose from: dial 1 for bill enquiries, 2 to upgrade his handset, 3 if he has a technical problem, 4 if he's thinking of leaving the company. From each of these he's taken through another list of options. If he still can't find what he is looking for, he's invited to 'stay on the line until an operator becomes available'. This can take up to ten minutes, by which time he is now seriously thinking of going back to option 4 and cancelling his contract. It really seems counter-productive.

C **Doug Cook, bank manager**
There is no doubt that modern communication channels have depersonalised a lot of customer contact. Banks have been doing this for years, trying to commoditise the service that they offer so that they can rationalise it and make it cheaper to deliver. Most transactions – bank deposits, cash withdrawals, issuing of statements – have been automated whether at a cash machine, over the phone or online. This has saved companies and the customer money. But cost-cutting is by no means the only driver – it's a trend also driven by customer demand for a quick and flexible service.

D **Farhana Patel, online retailer**
It's just about convenience. Whether I text you a message or tell you the same message face-to-face, it's still a message. The growth of Internet shopping compared to that of high street shopping shows very clearly that customers want cheaper and more accessible services. Sellers like the convenience too of course. eBay started out as a market place for individuals but, increasingly, companies have used it to sell products direct to consumers. In fact it's not very different from a traditional market place. There is still a community of buyers and sellers who talk to each other and do business just the same as if they were dealing face-to-face.

E **Brian MacWhinney, management consultant**
Businesses are often too quick to embrace new technology in order to save money or gain a competitive advantage. But applying the same solution to all types of business is never a good idea. There are cultural factors to consider. Using a call centre in India to handle enquiries about train times on railways in Europe is a bad idea because it isn't suited to customers' expectations. On the other hand, a European customer of a computer company doesn't really mind if his technical problem is solved by a call centre operator in India or Ireland or Alaska, because it doesn't require any cultural knowledge. Good communication is about finding the right channel. In time, I expect we'll see a return to more face-to-face contact with customers and more local services.

SPEAKING

1 **Which of the following do you find useful? When do you use it? Why?**

mobile phone email SMS MSN Blackberry

2 **Decide the best ways to communicate the following messages.**

What?	To whom?	How?
0 An apology for forgetting to send some information	A customer	Send a formal letter
1 The company's gratitude and appreciation	An employee who is about to retire	
2 A change of brand identity	The general public	
3 The appointment of a new managing director	All the employees	
4 A new website the company has created	Your customers	
5 The company's work to help the environment	The media and the general public	
6 Vacant posts for trainee salesmen and women	Young recruits	
7 A discount (for a limited period) on a product line	Your customers	
8 An apology for forgetting to send some information	A colleague	
9 The company's half-yearly financial results	The shareholders and financial institutions	

VOCABULARY

3 **Complete each definition with the correct word (the first letter has been written for you).**

0 To answer somebody, you give a reply.
1 To ask for something, you make a **r**_________ .
2 To help someone remember, you give them a **r**_________ .
3 To suggest or recommend something, you make a **p**_________ .
4 To say something publicly, you make an **a**_________ .
5 To say sorry you make an **a**_________ .
6 To insist that someone does something, you make a **d**_________ .

GRAMMAR

Grammar Tip

Often verbs that express a similar notion will take the same form, eg *dissuade, discourage, deter* are all followed by *someone from doing*.

This can also be the case with opposite notions, eg *agree* and *refuse + to do*.

I discouraged him from applying for the job.

I dissuaded him from applying for the job.

Verb patterns

4 **In the email below, all the forms following the communication verbs (*discuss, apologise*, etc) are underlined. Some are incorrect. Correct them.**

Dear Jim

First of all, I would like to thank you (**0**) ~~about giving~~ for giving up your time to help us. It's very kind of you to agree (**1**) working with us on this project – I know you are very busy.

When we last met, we discussed (**2**) about creating a special team to deal with complaints from customers. I have since had a meeting with Sarah, the head of the Customer Services team, and I have persuaded her (**3**) to join us. She suggested (**4**) to meet next week to put a plan in place. In the meantime, she is going to encourage her team (**5**) for giving their ideas.

I must just tell (**6**) to you something which happened last week that shows how much we need a better system for dealing with complaints.

Last week, a customer rang to complain (**7**) about having to wait one month for delivery of a DVD player. He accused us (**8**) to keep his money so that we could earn interest on it before delivering the product. The sales person who answered the call offered (**9**) giving him a discount, without even checking the history of the order. When I checked, I discovered an email from us informing the customer when he bought the product (**10**) that there will be a one-month delay in delivery. The salesman was very defensive and said that he couldn't be criticised (**11**) of trying to keep the customer happy!!

So you see, we've got a lot of work to do. Looking forward to hearing from you.

Best wishes
Karen

PS Remind me (**12**) to pay for lunch next time!

5 **Put the words below into their correct place in the table.**

urge threaten propose undertake praise
blame recommend deny convince

persuade + someone + *to do*	*promise* + *to do*	*admit* + *doing*	*criticise* + someone *for doing*	*suggest* + *doing* / *suggest that* someone *should do*
______	______	______	______	______
______	______	______	______	______
______	______	______	______	______

6 **Complete these sentences.**

0 They threatened *to take us to court* if we didn't pay them immediately.
1 It's a very sensitive issue. I suggest ______ an anonymous email.
2 Once, in a restaurant, I complained ______ and the manager told us to leave.
3 What a waste of time! We spent three hours discussing ______ .
4 The company offered ______ , but amazingly she refused.
5 I've promised ______ by tomorrow morning.
6 I can't believe you had to remind him ______ . That's his job!
7 The regulator accused the company ______ in its advertisements.

GRAMMAR

1 **Talk about one of the situations 1–4, answering the following questions. Remember to use the correct verb patterns.**

- When did it take place?
- What happened?
- Who was there?
- What was said?

1 an unusual presentation or talk that you attended
2 a memorable job interview you had
3 a meeting where two people disagreed strongly
4 an interesting business proposition that was made to you

*When I was in my final year of university, a friend **asked me** if I wanted to join him in a new business venture. Before I could **agree to do it**, I had to be sure that it was …*

LISTENING

Dealing with problems

2 **Look at this customer charter published on the website of *Penco Telecommunications*. How is it intended to make you feel about the company? Do you believe their promises?**

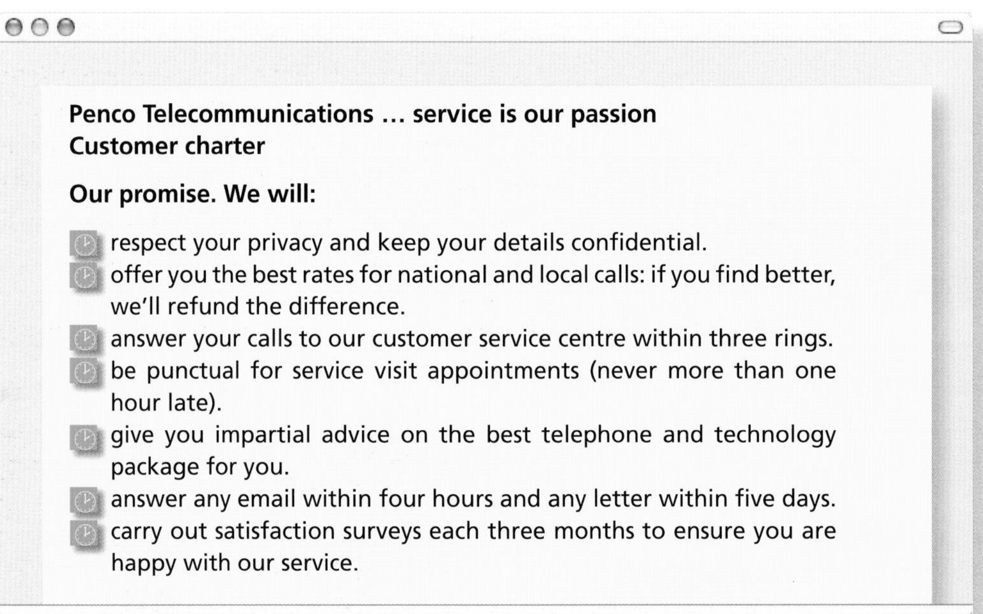

Penco Telecommunications … service is our passion
Customer charter

Our promise. We will:

- respect your privacy and keep your details confidential.
- offer you the best rates for national and local calls: if you find better, we'll refund the difference.
- answer your calls to our customer service centre within three rings.
- be punctual for service visit appointments (never more than one hour late).
- give you impartial advice on the best telephone and technology package for you.
- answer any email within four hours and any letter within five days.
- carry out satisfaction surveys each three months to ensure you are happy with our service.

3 3.1 **Listen to this phone conversation between an angry customer and a call centre operator for *Penco Telecommunications*.**

1 What is the customer's problem?
2 What solutions does the operator suggest?
3 Which one does the customer accept?

4 3.1 **Listen again and complete the phrases that the operator uses to deal sensitively and efficiently with the problem. Use 1–3 words for each space.**

1 I ____________________ the wait, sir.
2 Can I have your number and I ____________________ it straightaway?
3 Don't worry, I'll ____________________ to you.
4 He can be there by 6pm. ____________________ convenient?
5 I ____________________ understand. In ____________________, I'm going to have to reschedule him for another day.
6 I ____________________ what I can do. Please just ____________________ for a moment.
7 Would that be ____________________?
8 If you ____________________ tell me your mobile number, I can get that activated immediately.

SPEAKING

Handling calls sensitively

5 **Work with a partner. Take it in turns to make the call or receive the call. Study each situation and then act out the telephone conversation. Deal sensitively with each problem. Look at the notes below and prepare your telephone calls.**

Student A

1 You work for a parcel delivery company. Your computers have been behaving strangely today. Receive the call from a customer.
2 You ordered a fish tank from a mail order company. The picture in the catalogue showed a complete fish tank with heater, air pump and fish. But when it arrived it was just a glass box. Telephone to complain.
3 It is 6.30 in the evening. You receive a call from someone that you don't know. You don't like receiving unsolicited calls at home.
4 You work in the service department of an electricity company. You receive a request which is not really possible to satisfy.

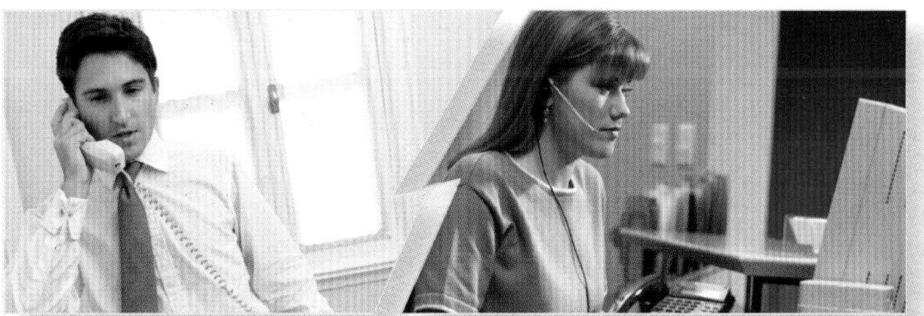

Student B

1 You have ordered delivery of a new laptop computer. When you track the order on the internet, you find that it has gone from Ireland to Hong Kong. You live in London. Telephone to find out what's happening.
2 You work for a mail order company that supplies aquariums and accessories. You receive a call from an unhappy and confused customer.
3 You work for a promotions company for a fitness club. You call potential customers in the evenings to offer them a free month's trial of their local gym. Make the call.
4 While at work you suddenly realise that you have left your iron on at home – in a small village one hour's drive away. Telephone the electricity company to see if they can cut off the electricity supply to your house.

3.2 Email exchange

WRITING

Formal and informal emails

Writing styles

The style of a business email or letter depends on the occasion for writing and the relationship with the receiver.

1 They can be formal:
Please find attached our proposal. I would be grateful if you could check it and send us confirmation of your acceptance.
2 They can be more conversational:
Attached is our proposal. Please check it and confirm that you are happy with it.
3 Emails can sometimes be in a kind of shorthand:
Pls check the attached proposal and confirm

1 Highlight the differences between the formal and informal emails below. Discuss the differences with your partner.

Formal

Dear Mr Scott
Thank you very much for your letter introducing your company. Currently, we do not have any demand for marketing consultancy. However, this situation could change in the future and therefore I will certainly keep your details on file. In the meantime, I would be grateful if you could send us an up-to-date list of your fees.
Once again, thank you for your interest.
Yours sincerely
Monica Stuuf

Informal

Dear James
Thanks for the information about your company. At the moment, we're not really looking for any help with marketing consultancy, but we might be in the future, so I'll certainly hang on to your details. For now, please send us an up-to-date list of your fees.
Thanks again for your interest.
Kind regards
Monica Stuuf

2 For sentences 1–4 write the contracted forms in full and for 5–8 write the contracted form.

1 I'll let you know tomorrow.
2 I'd like an answer asap.
3 I won't know till Friday.
4 I can't help you, I'm afraid.
5 It has been ages since I have seen him.
6 I would have told you if I had known.
7 I should not be surprised if they are late.
8 You must not do anything until I say so.

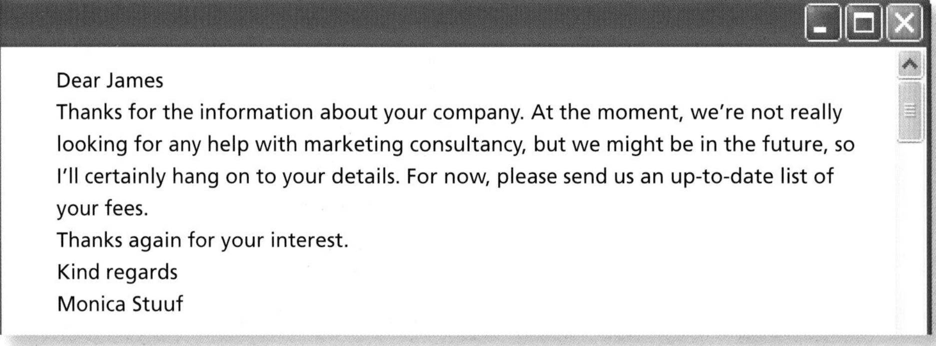

3 Match each formal linking word on the left with its neutral equivalent on the right.

1 however	so
2 nevertheless	because of
3 consequently	after
4 owing to	because
5 moreover	anyway
6 following	but
7 since	what's more
8 besides	still

Exam Success

Before writing, always think carefully about your relationship to the target reader. Adapt the tone and style of your letter or email accordingly.

4 Rewrite the following informal email to a customer as a more formal one. Use the expressions in the box to help you.

I would be grateful if   contact   further to   do not hesitate   in agreement with
however   strictly speaking   please find attached   Yours sincerely

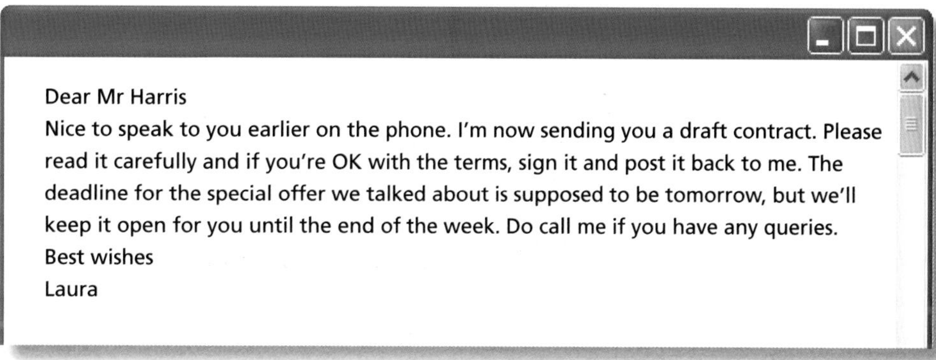
Dear Mr Harris
Nice to speak to you earlier on the phone. I'm now sending you a draft contract. Please read it carefully and if you're OK with the terms, sign it and post it back to me. The deadline for the special offer we talked about is supposed to be tomorrow, but we'll keep it open for you until the end of the week. Do call me if you have any queries.
Best wishes
Laura

5 Welcon has supplied receptionists and doormen for your company's headquarters for over five years. Recently the standard of service they give has declined sharply. Visitors have complained about rudeness, being kept waiting and being misdirected. Write an email to the company:

- emphasising the good relationship you have had in the past.
- describing the unacceptable behaviour of their staff recently.
- insisting that changes are made immediately.

6 Send the email to your partner. When you have exchanged, read each other's emails and then write a reply.

3.3

Listening Test: Introduction and Part One

EXAM FORMAT

The Listening Test has three parts, in which there are a total of 30 questions, and lasts approximately 40 minutes. It carries 25% of the total marks.

Part	Listening type	Task
1	One 3–4-minute monologue Played twice	Gap-filling (up to three words or a number)
2	Five short monologues Played twice	Two different tasks matching each monologue to, for example, the topic described, the reason for speaking, the opinion of the speaker, etc
3	One 4–5-minute conversation Played twice	Answer multiple choice comprehension questions (three choices: A, B and C)

You will have ten minutes at the end of the test to transfer your answers to an answer sheet.

Exam Success

Useanytimeyouare given before the recording starts to read the questions and to anticipate the context and meaning of what you are about to hear.

APPROACH

Part One

Follow these steps.

- Read the instructions twice and make sure you understand the context of the passage and what you are being asked to do.
- In particular, check how many words you can put into each gap.
- Try to put yourself in the situation of the audience to generate a real interest.
- Read through the questions and try to predict the type of word that will go into each gap.
- Never leave a gap empty.

KEY SKILL

Prediction

1 Look at these sentences and try to predict what kind of word(s) will go into each space.

The background

1 The company was set up in ______________ .

2 The project has been funded by the Ministry of ______________ .

The job

3 The post is open to ______________ .

4 You don't need to have ______________ .

5 You will be expected to ______________ .

What to do next

6 Candidates should apply ______________ .

7 The deadline for applications is ______________ .

EXAM PRACTICE

2 3.2 **Following the approach described on page 34 do Practice Test Part One. Take two minutes to study the instructions and sentences before the tape begins.**

PART ONE

Questions 1–12

- You are going to hear part of a one-day seminar entitled 'A career in coaching'. The head of the Coaching Academy is talking to participants about his organisation and what coaching involves.
- As you listen, complete the notes using up to three words or a number in each space.
- You will hear the recording twice.

A CAREER IN COACHING

The Coaching Academy

1 The Coaching Academy was established in ....

2 The academy doesn't receive ....

3 The aim of the academy is to ....

4 Training courses at the academy last from .... to four weeks.

What is coaching?

5 Coaches offer help to people in their business and ....

6 The basic principles are always the same: to build people's self-belief and help them ....

7 Coaches try to help the client to look ....

8 Counselling often focuses more on .... in people's lives.

Qualifications and rewards

9 When you can make a difference to someone's life it gives you great ....

10 The basic rate of pay for a coach is about ....

11 Apart from doing a course in coaching you will need .... in the field you are coaching in.

12 Some coaches conduct coaching sessions by phone, online or even sometimes ....

4.1 The art of selling

VOCABULARY

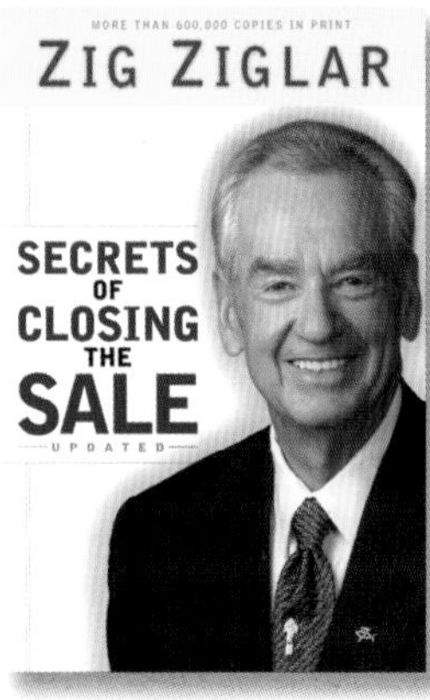

Selling

1 What do these quotations suggest are the qualities of a successful salesman?

'Your attitude, not your aptitude, will determine your altitude.'
'People don't buy for logical reasons. They buy for emotional reasons.'
'Failure is a detour, not a dead-end street.'
'People often say that motivation doesn't last. Well, neither does bathing – that's why we recommend it daily.'
'The complaining customer represents a huge opportunity for more business.'
Zig Ziglar, author of *Secrets of Closing the Sale*

2 Have you ever sold anything? Do you consider yourself to be good at selling? Why? / Why not?

3 Complete this short article about the importance of selling using the words given below.

prospective emotional unique competitive
~~price~~ maker added after-sales

There is so much competition in the market place today, particularly **(0)** price competition, that it is unusual for a seller to be able to find a **(1)** ______________ selling point or a **(2)** ______________ advantage with which to convince the customer. Instead he has to rely on using **(3)** ______________ benefits and/or giving **(4)** ______________ value to the customer through **(5)** ______________ service. This makes the job of the seller all the more important. What he has to do is identify the real decision **(6)** ______________ in the buying process and then act quickly on a buying signal. A buying signal is when the **(7)** ______________ customer gives a sign to the seller that he is open to being sold the product or service.

4 Look at these statements by different prospective buyers of a car. Imagine you are the sales person at a car dealer's dealing with them. What would you say or do next to try to close the sale?

1 'I really like the car, but it's a bit outside my budget.'
2 'It's got everything I want, but silver is not the colour I had in mind.'
3 'I'm really confused about all these extra options – I just wanted to buy a car, not a spaceship!'
4 'Thank you for your time. I'm going to go away and think about it.'
5 'I've always had a VW. I don't know if this car suits my image.'

LISTENING

Sales techniques

5 **Work with your partner. Make a list of the main reasons for a customer deciding not to buy a product or service.**

6 **Compare your answer with Zig Ziglar's on page 127.**

7 4.1 **Listen to an extract from a radio series *At Work*, where people talk about their working experiences. In this programme two sales people describe their approach to selling.**

1 What are they selling?
2 What is the approach of each?
3 What are the advantages and disadvantages of each approach?

8 4.1 **Look at these extracts from the programme and complete the gaps. Listen again to check your answers.**

1 Competition is ______________ – not necessarily price competition, because in our sector, quality, ______________ and service are far more important factors.
2 We use a sales ______________ that's called 'relationship selling'.
3 We spend a lot of time getting to know each ______________ individual needs.
4 I have to freely admit to people that our products may not be best ______________ to their particular needs.
5 I'd much prefer to be doing that than using some ______________ technique.
6 In my line of business, it's all about ____________ benefits.
7 It's difficult to ______________ any kind of technical competitive advantage for long.
8 I deal only with the decision maker, who's generally a ______________ for a chain of stores.
9 ... the most expensive options, because this increases our ______________ sales.
10 As soon as I get a buying signal from them, ... I ______________ in and close the sale ...
11 ... by discussing quantities required, special delivery arrangements, ______________ payment terms.

9 **What are the main advantages and disadvantages of the sales promotion media below? Consider the following criteria in your evaluation.**

- cost
- reach (how many see it)
- consumer perception
- mass or niche (targeted advertising)
- success rate
- impact

Medium	Advantages	Disadvantages
1 Radio advertisements		
2 Point-of-sale promotion		
3 Sponsorship of a sports event		
4 Direct mail (by post or email)		
5 Word-of-mouth recommendation		
6 Billboards (in town or on main roads)		
7 Viral marketing (over the Internet)		
8 Vehicle advertising (company or public)		

READING

Advertising trends

1 **Read the headline on page 39 and predict what the article will say about advertising trends.**

2 **Read the text quickly. Were you correct in your prediction? Do you agree with the author's analysis?**

3 **Study the text again to find the best answer (A, B, C or D) to each question.**

1 According to the author changes are occurring in
   A the types of television programme we watch.
   B the way people, especially young people, access video.
   C the way televisions are made.
   D the amount of programmes that are recorded.

2 2005 was a significant year for television in the UK because
   A it was the year Internet use overtook television viewing.
   B spending on TV advertising declined.
   C viewing figures peaked and started to decline.
   D the 16 to 24 age group watched more television than before.

3 In the future, big global companies will
   A move away from TV to alternative advertising media.
   B still use television to establish their brands.
   C try to target their advertisements more precisely.
   D return to non-broadcast methods like direct mailing.

4 The growing use of PVRs means that television viewers
   A skip through the advertisements without looking at them.
   B are exposed to a bigger range of advertisements.
   C can get advertising on demand.
   D can pause and rewind advertisements.

5 The other growing area of opportunity for advertisers is
   A outdoor advertising.
   B ice dancing.
   C big live sporting events.
   D football.

6 The trend for on-demand viewing of programmes
   A represents a big threat for advertisers.
   B means advertisers will spend a lot of money to reach a clear target audience.
   C will challenge search-based advertising on the Internet.
   D will increase agencies advertising revenues.

7 Advertisers in the future will ask their agencies to attract the young
   A with a range of new Internet-based media.
   B with more friendly messages.
   C through chat rooms.
   D using computer viruses.

THE AD REVOLUTION WILL NOT BE TELEVISED

Among most advertisers, agencies and media companies there is a growing consensus that the old broadcast models of advertising are being eroded by the march of technology and that new models will have to be found to promote their products.

Consider the growing ubiquity of broadband access and the digital revolution that is fragmenting television viewing across hundreds of channels. Then combine those trends with the upsurge in personal video recorder technology (PVR) and the tendency for younger viewers to watch less TV in favour of sharing their own words, pictures, music and movies online.

In the UK, television viewing fell in 2005 for the first time in the medium's history. The decline was most pronounced among those aged 16 to 24. In the US, where broadband penetration is even more widespread, those under 25 now spend more time on the Internet than watching television. The effect of these changing media habits is now having a material effect on advertising spending.

But according to Neil Jones of media agency, Carat UK, and others at the sharp end, big companies like Coca Cola and Unilever are actively reducing the amount they spend on television in favour of boosting their Internet budgets and so-called 'direct response' advertising – anything from online viral ads to traditional mail campaigns.

Unilever, the consumer goods giant, has said that during the last five years around a fifth of its £300m ad budget was shifted out of television and into outdoor posters, online advertising and sponsorship, such as Flora's long-running association with the London Marathon. Meanwhile, the PVR effect is starting to make its presence felt now that the devices, which allow viewers to easily record shows as well as pause and rewind live TV, are in a meaningful number of homes. Over 1.3 million people now use the technology, with the majority fast forwarding through adverts on recorded shows.

Increased broadband penetration and download speeds are only likely to accelerate the trend for on-demand viewing. Channel 4 chief executive Andy Duncan recently forecast that by 2016 'the majority of all programmes will be consumed in an on-demand way, whether through personal video recorders or video-on-demand over the Internet'. As the boom in search-based advertising on the Internet has proved, if advertisers are sure that they are accurately targeting a receptive audience they will pay a huge premium. Meanwhile event television, which viewers will tune in to watch live, and could be anything from the World Cup to *Dancing on Ice*, will become increasingly vital.

As a result of these trends the amount spent on traditional television advertising on the main channels is declining, while the amount spent on the web is booming. Advertising experts are agreed that brands will increasingly have to engage with individual consumers rather than hoping to catch their attention with traditional catch-all ads.

Advertisers are demanding a more holistic view from their agencies, asking them to consider how to tap into younger consumers via blogs, social networking sites, advertiser-funded content and viral advertising. The latter, which involves making branded messages so engaging and interesting that web users feel compelled to send them on to friends, has come of age during the past two years. 'We're seeing a new wave of interest because brands are looking for new forms of media and new marketing techniques,' says Will Jeffery, Managing Director of viral advertising agency Maverick.

In the short term, Hassell, director at digital agency Ralph, believes that advertisers will increasingly release adverts on the Internet first as a means of creating a buzz around a particular clip.

GRAMMAR

Tenses and time phrases

1 Which tense would you expect to follow each of the time phrases below?

present simple   present continuous   present perfect
will   future perfect   past simple

1 Up to now ...
2 A few years ago ...
3 At the moment ...
4 By the year 2050 ...
5 Nowadays ...
6 Over the past ten years ...
7 In the next five years ...
8 During the 1980s ...
9 Sooner or later ...

2 Use the appropriate time phrase from exercise 1 to complete each sentence.

1 ____________________ we have seen a gradual reduction in working hours.
2 ____________________ no-one has found a satisfactory solution to the problem of the ageing population.
3 ____________________ watching television was more popular among younger age groups than using the Internet.
4 ____________________ the advertising industry enjoyed a boom.
5 ____________________ the economy will begin to recover from its recent downturn.
6 ____________________ global temperatures will have risen by 3°C.
7 ____________________ politicians pay too much attention to presentation of their policies and too little attention to their substance.

3 Write some sentences of your own using the time phrases from exercise 1.

GRAMMAR

Transitive and intransitive verbs

4 Choose the correct verb to complete each sentence.

1 The government is going to *rise / raise* the school leaving age from 16 to 17.
2 The price of oil has *risen / raised* again.
3 Sales have *reduced / fallen* in the last two months.
4 You will have to *reduce / fall* the price to attract ordinary working people.

What are the grammatical differences between the pairs of words?

5 In which of the sentences in exercise 4 would the following verbs fit?

↑ increase   go up   put up   soar
↓ cut   go down   drop   decrease   lower   collapse

6 Use one of the verbs (transitive or intransitive) to describe the following things in your country.

1 house prices
2 the gap between rich and poor
3 taxes
4 the cost of living in general

SPEAKING

In the field

7 **As a sales rep for a medium-sized Italian company, you are visiting shops and department stores in Denmark to persuade them to stock your designer lamps.**

- Work with a partner. Take the roles of sales rep and buyer for a shop. Look at the situations below and plan what each will say.
- Act out the conversations following the example. Try to use at least one of the verbs (*rise, lower*, etc) in your conversation.

0 The shop buyer only has a few Italian catalogues.
Shop buyer: People drop into the shop all the time to pick up catalogues, but you've only sent us ten and they're all written in Italian.
Sales rep: We can certainly increase the number of catalogues we send you, but until the volume of sales goes up, it's not economical to publish them in Danish.

1 The buyer wants to place a small order (four or five) as a trial, but the prices are too high.
2 The buyer loves the lamps, but wants a shorter delivery time on orders. Customers won't wait three to four weeks.
3 The shop normally marks up prices by 100%, but in this case that will make the price to the customer too high.
4 The buyer likes the lamps but feels very loyal to existing suppliers.
5 The buyer needs more point-of-sale promotional material – displays, catalogues, etc.

WRITING

A sales report

8 **During your sales trip to Denmark you receive the following email from your boss.**

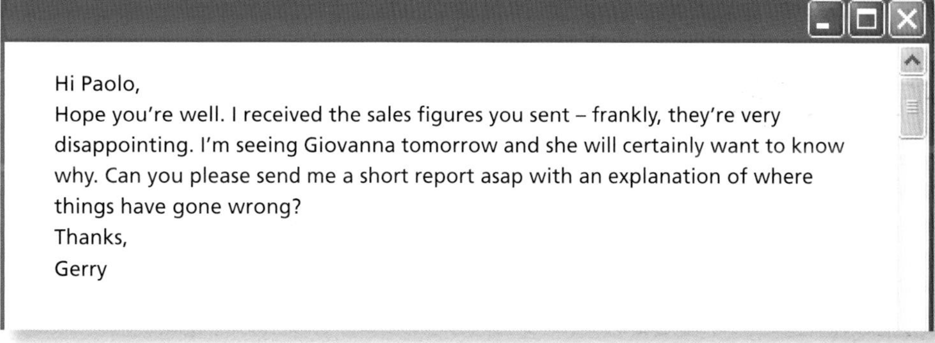

Hi Paolo,
Hope you're well. I received the sales figures you sent – frankly, they're very disappointing. I'm seeing Giovanna tomorrow and she will certainly want to know why. Can you please send me a short report asap with an explanation of where things have gone wrong?
Thanks,
Gerry

Using the framework below and expanding the notes in italics, write a sales report (200 words approx).

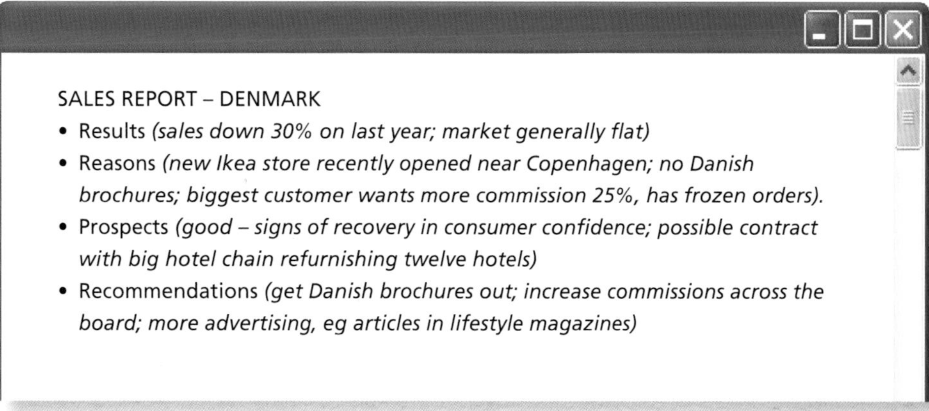

SALES REPORT – DENMARK

- Results *(sales down 30% on last year; market generally flat)*
- Reasons *(new Ikea store recently opened near Copenhagen; no Danish brochures; biggest customer wants more commission 25%, has frozen orders).*
- Prospects *(good – signs of recovery in consumer confidence; possible contract with big hotel chain refurnishing twelve hotels)*
- Recommendations *(get Danish brochures out; increase commissions across the board; more advertising, eg articles in lifestyle magazines)*

.2 Presenting figures

VOCABULARY

Describing performance

1 The following six elements are important when describing performance.

- time phrases — *In the last five years* our sales have remained fairly stable.
- verbs — At the same time our direct costs *have risen.*
- nouns — This *increase* has put pressure on our margins.
- prepositions — In response we have cut expenditure *by* about 15%.
- qualifiers — There has also been a *slight* increase in productivity.
- cause and result — *As a result,* our margins have actually improved.

2 Think of words that could replace the underlined words in this sales figures presentation about bicycle sales.

It's been a roller coaster of a year with bicycle sales (**1**) going up and down unpredictably. After a poor start to the year – post-Christmas blues, I guess – sales (**2**) picked up in February and hit a (**3**) high point in March, which is very early, compared to other years. It was probably (**4**) due to the unusually warm weather, but who knows? Anyway (**5**) the result was that production had to go into overdrive to get the products out. (**6**) Over the next three months, things (**7**) stabilised and in July, when we normally do very well, sales actually dropped (**8**) a bit. At that point, we decided to clear out our stock and started offering reductions in the retail price of bikes of (**9**) up to 40%. The strategy worked amazingly well and (**10**) resulted in a dramatic increase in sales, even though our margins (**11**) fell.

3 Use these words to replace those underlined in the sales figures presentation in exercise 2. Were your suggestions different?

it meant   led to   sharp   recovered   following   levelled off   peak
as much as   during   decreased   fluctuating   because of   slightly

LISTENING

A sales forecast

4 4.2 **Rexil AG manufactures and sells pharmaceutical products. Anticipating customers' needs (demand forecasting) provides vital information for the production and distribution divisions of the company. You will hear Anke Reigl present her forecast for sales of best-selling product, HAB, over the next six months. Listen and complete the notes taken at the meeting.**

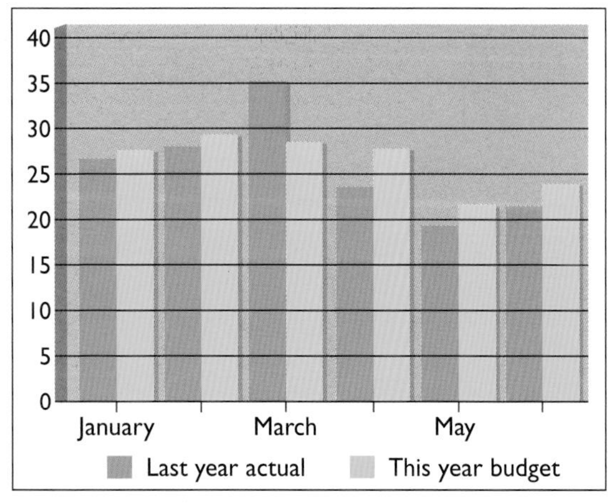

Sales forecast for HAB – 1st half

1 First quarter: 2–3% increase predicted, based on ____________.

2 Second quarter: 7–10% increase following ____________.

3 March figure lower, because last year's high sales due to ____________.

4 Sales will decline in April and May – reason is ____________.

5 April much higher this year because of ____________.

SPEAKING

Presenting figures

Exam Success

In presentations, involve your audience as much as possible:

- relatethesubject totheirexperience
- ask rhetorical questions
- invitequestions; use humour
- maintain eye contact

5 **You are going to give a sales presentation. Choose one of the sales graphs below for your presentation.**

- Note down possible reasons for the developments in the graph.
- Give your presentation describing the development and the reasons.

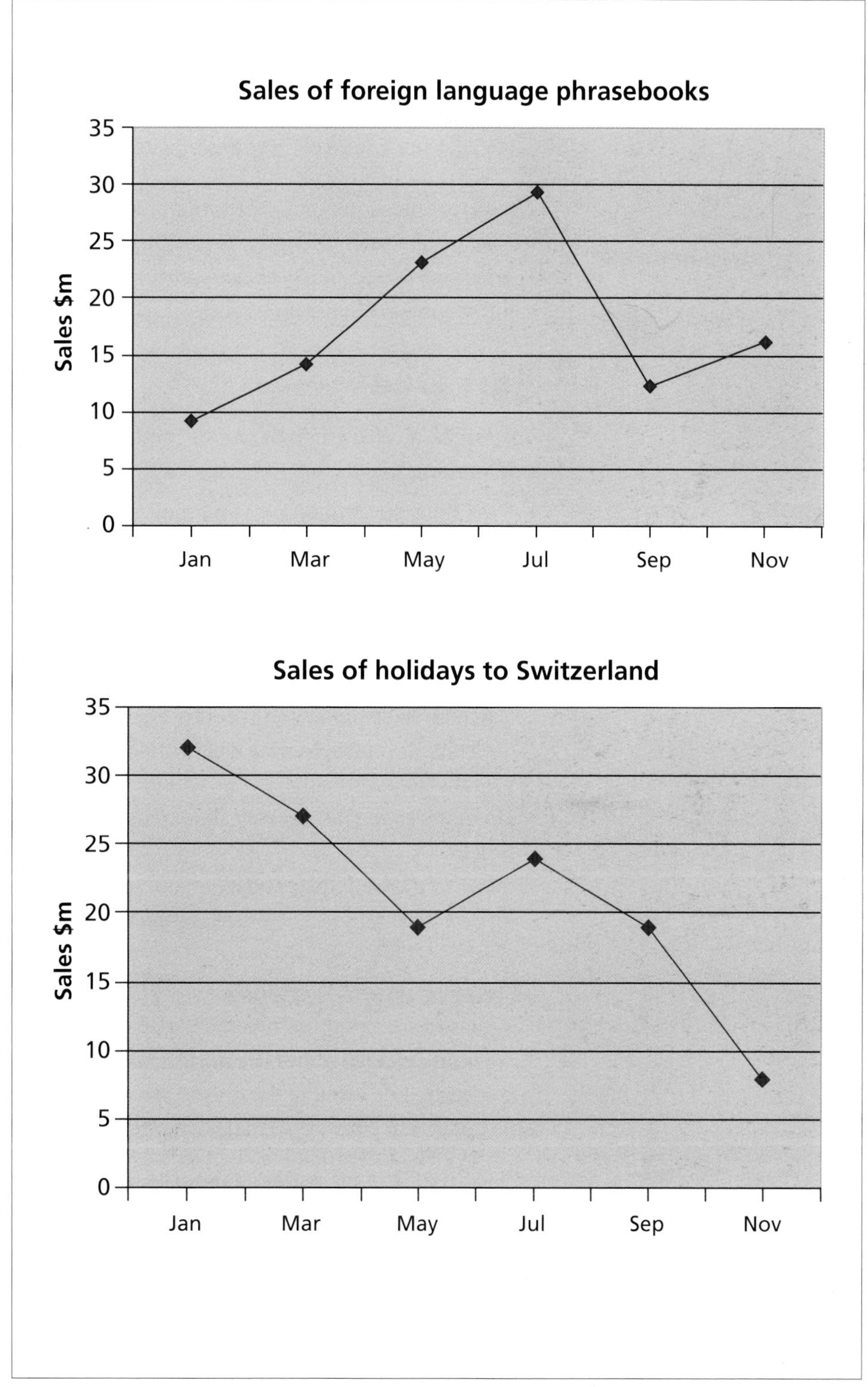

4.3

Writing Test: Introduction and Part One

EXAM FORMAT

The Writing Test has two parts, in which there are a total of four questions (you must answer two), and lasts one hour ten minutes. It carries 25% of the total marks.

Part	Writing task	Length
1	Describing and explaining a graph	120–140 words
2	Choose one of three types: a letter, report or proposal	200–250 words

For all the question types the examiner is looking at your answer for:
- a clear sense of the purpose for writing, and content which realises the task.
- conciseness and clarity of expression.
- an awareness of the target reader, and appropriate style and formality.

Exam Success

Trytoputyourselfin the shoes of the writer; get interested in the topic and imagine this is a real business writing task, not an exam exercise.

APPROACH

Part One

You will be given a graph or pair of graphs to analyse, explain and comment on. Follow these steps.

- Read the instructions twice and make sure you understand what you are being asked to do.
- Study the graph(s) and decide what general trends they show and what you can conclude from these. Make short notes to help you.
- Write the report with the following structure:
  - an introduction (explaining the subject matter of the graphs)
  - a main body (describing and comparing each development in general terms)
  - a conclusion (explaining what conclusions can be drawn from the facts presented in the graphs)
- Do not describe the development of the curves in year-by-year or month-by-month detail.
- When you have finished go over your text and check for basic grammatical errors, eg consistency in use of tenses, subject–verb agreement, spelling mistakes.

KEY SKILL

Analysing a graph

1 Here is an example about the number of vehicles per capita of the world's population. Look first at the graph. What are the main trends? What will be the effect of this in your view? Make brief notes on what you are going to say.

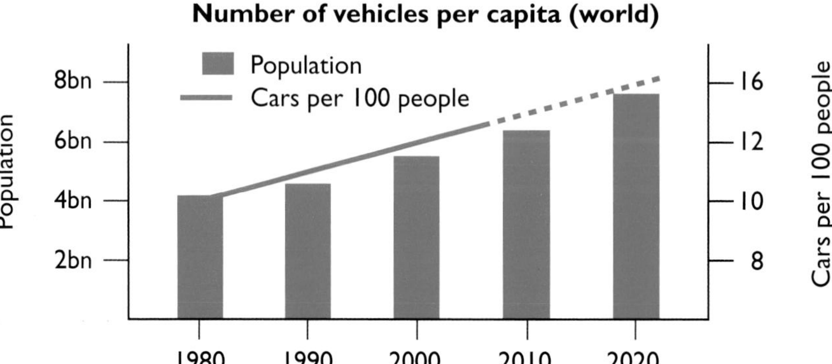

2 **Compare these notes with your own.**

- Steady rise in population (4.2bn to 7.7bn)
- Rise in number of vehicles over same period 10% to 16%
- Total number of vehicles more than double
- Impact on oil reserves and pollution?

3 **Read this report analysing the graph in exercise 1 on page 44. What do you note about:**

1 how it is structured?

2 the amount of detail in which the developments are described?

The graph shows the number of cars per 100 people over the period 1980 to 2020 relative to the growth of the world's population.

If we look first at the growth in population, we can see there is a steady increase from 4.2 billion people in 1980 to 7.7 billion in 2020, with the most significant increase coming between 2000 and 2020. The number of vehicles per 100 people follows a similar trend, rising steadily over the same period. From ten cars per 100 people in 1980 it is projected to increase to sixteen in 2020.

The dramatic consequence of these two developments when combined is that the total number of vehicles almost doubles in 40 years, a fact which is certain to have implications for energy resources and pollution in the future.

EXAM PRACTICE

4 **Following the approach described above, answer the following Practice Test Part One.**

PART ONE

- The graph below shows the supply and demand for palm oil (the main ingredient in hand soap) over the period 1985 to 2006.
- Using the information in the graph, write a short **report** describing supply and demand and the relation between the two.
- Write **120–140** words.

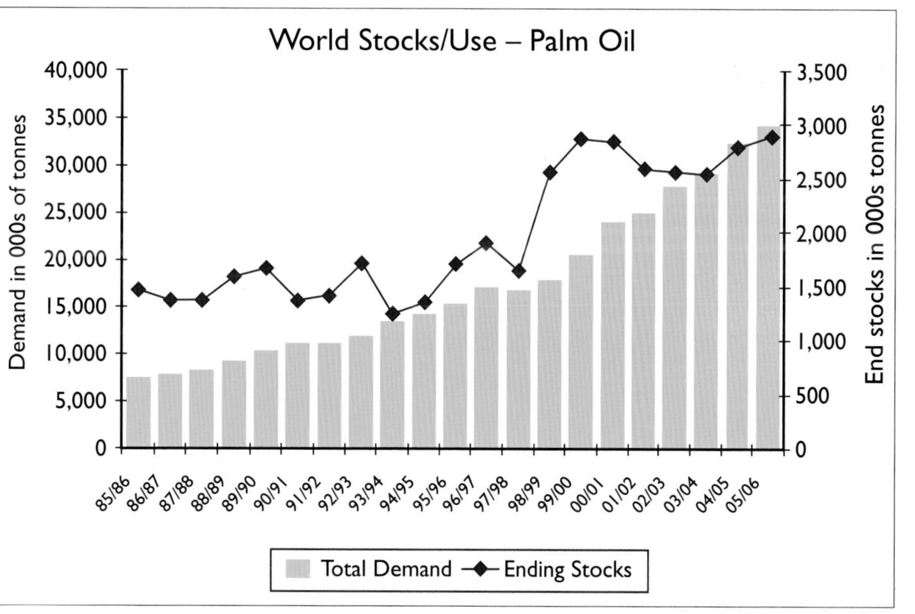

5.1 Money and finance

VOCABULARY

Money expressions

1 How do you interpret this quotation?

'Money often costs too much.'
Ralph Waldo Emerson, Essayist

2 Complete these flow charts. Use the words in the box.

do	invest	save	~~earn~~	withdraw	
owe	bet	repay	invoiced	do	lend

0 *earn* money →be paid for your work →spend money
1 borrow money →________ money →pay back money
2 ________ money →charge interest →make a profit
3 order goods →be ________ for the goods →pay for the goods
4 ________ money on a horse →win money →collect your winnings
5 ________ money in shares →earn interest →buy more shares
6 go to the bank →________ some money →spend the money
7 put your car up for sale →receive an offer →________ a deal
8 find a car you want to buy →negotiate a discount →________ money
9 ________ business →make a profit →reinvest the profit
10 be short of money →take out a loan →________ the loan

3 What's the difference between the following?

1 *win* money and *earn* money
2 *lend* and *borrow* money
3 *spend* and *waste* money
4 *costs* and *is worth* £300

SPEAKING

A bank loan

4 Work with a partner. Take the roles of bank manager and loan applicant and act out the conversation. Look at the notes and plan what you are going to say.

Bank manager	**Loan applicant**
You must decide if you are able to lend the money to the applicant. Find out: • about his / her financial situation (salary, other income, savings, main outgoings, other debts). • what the loan is for. Be prepared to give details of interest rates, terms of the loan, security needed, etc.	You need to borrow some money. Be prepared to say: • what you want to buy, how much money you need and for how long. • what your financial situation is (salary, other income, savings, main outgoings, other debts). Also find out about the interest rates and other terms of the loan.

LISTENING

A culture of debt

5 **Discuss these questions.**

1 Is it easy to get credit in your country, for example, to buy a house, a car, a new TV?
2 Is consumer confidence high at the moment? Why? / Why not?
3 What is people's general attitude to borrowing in your country?

Exam Success

Youranswerswillbe exact word-for-word phrases from the listening text. They must be spelt correctly.

6 **You will hear part of a lecture given by an economist to a group of bankers and economists. In it she describes the impact of Alan Greenspan's economic policy on the US and global economies. A friend who can't attend has asked you to take some notes. Before listening predict the kind of words that will go in each space.**

7 5.1 **Listen and complete the notes below. Use up to three words in each space.**

Business **MAGAZINE**

THE LEGACY OF ALAN GREENSPAN

The background

1 Alan Greenspan changed people's attitudes to ________________ .

2 People have been against borrowing money since ________________ .

3 Now young people take out loans to pay their way through ____________ .

4 For many homeowners it's normal to have a second ________________ .

The current lending market

5 Credit is easy and interest rates are ________________ .

6 Banks often lend money ________________ .

7 In some states it's possible to get a mortgage with no ________________ .

Reasons for this policy

8 As long as people are spending, ________________ .

9 In Germany, in times of uncertainty people tend to ________________ .

The future

10 In 2005 American personal debt was ________________ .

11 Some people say we are sitting on ________________ .

12 Asset values will not continue to rise ________________ .

8 **Do you think a policy of *borrow and spend* helps the economy? Or do you think sooner or later there will be a debt crisis?**

9 **Explain the following financial terms from the text.**

1 to remortgage your home
2 to make a down-payment
3 asset values will crash
4 to be in negative equity
5 64 trillion dollars

GRAMMAR

Expressions of comparison

1 Underline the expressions of comparison and the adverbs / prepositions that go with them.

0 Warsaw is cheaper than Oslo.
1 I find the train more comfortable than the bus.
2 Wal-mart is the biggest food retailer in the USA.
3 It's not as expensive as you think.
4 The two articles present the same arguments as each other.
5 Hungarian is a different language to German.
6 Australian food is similar to New Zealand's.
7 It took me less time than I thought it would.
8 The average American consumes twice as much energy as the average European.

2 What word(s) could you add to the statements in exercise 1 to show that the difference (or similarity) is big? Use these words to help you (sometimes there is more than one possibility).

much far by far over very exactly nearly completely

0 Warsaw is cheaper than Oslo.
Warsaw is much cheaper than Oslo.

3 Make comparisons (differences and similarities) between the following.

1 you and another member of your family (father, mother, brother, sister, etc)
2 two cities you know well
3 two employers or teachers you have had
4 your own country and another country you have visited
5 two companies you have worked for or colleges you have attended

4 Read this article about energy consumption in the USA. Write one word to fill each gap.

Energy consumption in the USA

Although the USA has only 5% of the world's population, it is **(0)** the largest consumer of energy **(1)** _________ far, consuming 26%. This is **(2)** _________ so surprising as it is also the world's largest industrialised economy. However, the USA does waste more energy **(3)** _________ other nations: gas-guzzling cars which consume **(4)** _________ more fuel than the average European or Asian car; planes which endlessly criss-cross the country. Indeed 28% of the USA's energy is consumed by transportation and **(5)** _________ all this transport uses oil for fuel. The standard for car fuel consumption in America today is **(6)** _________ the same as it was twenty years ago – 27.5 miles per gallon. **(7)** _________ last, however, there are moves by the government to control this consumption. Politicians are beginning to realise that, of all the players in the equation, it is consumers who have the **(8)** _________ leverage, not the oil suppliers.

SPEAKING

Choosing an investment

5 In the city where you live (180,000 people), two independent cinemas have recently come up for sale. Both are in a popular suburb of the city. The city has three other cinemas – a big out-of-town mutiplex, a six-screen cinema in the centre of town and a small independent in a different suburb.

The details of the two cinemas are given below. Study the information and decide which you think would be a better investment.

The Last Picture Palace

Location:	One mile from the city centre in popular student area
Seating capacity:	180 people
Parking facilities:	None
Current cost of a ticket:	£5
Lease:	15 years remaining; £15,000 p.a.
Turnover last year:	£110,000
Costs:	30% of ticket sales to distributor; salaries £35,000 p.a.; running costs £10,000 p.a.
Facilities:	None (ticket office and auditorium only)
Condition:	In need of repair and redecoration (£40,000 investment needed)
Price:	£40,000 (includes all fittings and cinema equipment)

The Regal Cinema

Location:	Two miles from the city centre on main road out of city
Seating capacity:	620 people
Parking facilities:	50 cars
Current cost of a ticket:	£6
Lease:	9 years remaining; £50,000 p.a.
Turnover last year:	£390,000 (made a loss)
Costs:	30% of ticket sales to distributor; salaries £130,000 p.a.; other overheads and taxes £85,000 p.a.
Facilities:	Single auditorium, food and drinks counter, bar
Condition:	In need of complete refurbishment to create two new auditoriums (£300,000 investment needed)
Price:	£1

6 Discuss your ideas with your partner, explaining your reasons. Use the language box to help you.

Stating preferences

Personally I'd go for option A because it's ...
I think option A has much more going for it. For a start, it's ...
My preference would be option A because ...
We would be better off buying option A, because ...
Option A offers better ...
The only disadvantage I can see is ...
I have several reservations about option B. Firstly, it's ...
I think option B has several drawbacks. It's ...
Option B, on the other hand, is too ...
All in all, option A represents the best solution because ...

VOCABULARY

Company finance

1 What financial mistakes do you think small businesses most commonly make? Work with a partner and make a list.

Not taking out insurance to cover the sudden loss of a senior / key employee.

2 Put these words into the right place to make pairs of financial terms.

long-term expenditure accounts receivable net ~~fixed costs~~
retained profit unprofitable loss debtor liabilities

0 variable costs fixed costs
1 income ______
2 assets ______
3 gross ______
4 current ______
5 profit ______
6 dividends ______
7 creditor ______
8 profitable ______
9 accounts payable ______

3 Using the words in exercise 2 complete this passage from an online guide for investors.

Guide for investors

Understanding financial statements

To make good investment decisions, you need to understand the business you're investing in. Knowing when to buy and when to sell depends not only on understanding the market in general but also the financial health of the company. Your first port of call: the annual report.

This contains the accounts – the balance sheet, the income statement and the cashflow statement. We'll deal with just the first two here because they are the most important. With all financial statements, you must compare the sets of figures from recent years to see how the company is developing.

The balance sheet is a snapshot of a company's financial position at a given moment. Imagine tomorrow you make a list of everything you own (including what others owe to you) – house, car, money in the bank, etc. These are your (**1**) ______ . Set against these everything that you owe – mortgage, credit card bills, etc. These are your (**2**) ______ . The two columns are what make up the balance sheet.

With a company balance sheet you also need to consider the shareholders' equity (the shares owned in the company by others). The basic equation is *assets = liabilities + shareholders' equity*.

The (**3**) ______ assets of a company are its buildings and equipment. As an investor you should pay particular attention to two kinds of current asset – the stock and the accounts receivable (money owed to the company by customers). If the amount of stock is growing fast, then it could be that stock isn't moving. If the accounts receivable figure is large, then the (**4**) ______ aren't paying their bills quickly enough. On the liability side look to see whether the debt, both short and long term, is increasing. Is the company borrowing more and if so, why? Read the notes to the accounts – maybe they will explain anything unusual. Look also at accounts (**5**) ______ to see if the company is paying its creditors on time.

The income statement (sometimes also called the profit and (**6**) ______ account) shows the company's income and (**7**) ______ over a given period. It lists all the money generated by sales (the turnover) plus any other income, minus all the costs involved in running the business. This produces the gross profit that tells you if the business is healthy and operationally (**8**) ______ . (**9**) ______ profit is the proverbial bottom line. It represents profit after tax and interest have been paid and is the amount that can be distributed to its shareholders in (**10**) ______ (though generally a part of this profit is retained for re-investment).

As you study the income statements of recent years, get out your calculator and do some sums.
Are sales growing? Are costs growing faster than sales or is the profit margin being maintained? What are the forecasts for future growth? Did any of the income come from the sales of assets?

4 **What do these words and phrases from the passage on page 50 mean?**

1 your first port of call
2 a snapshot
3 over a given period
4 the bottom line
5 do some sums

READING

A financial summary

5 **Study this financial summary of Tesco plc, Britain's largest supermarket chain. Find the following items.**

1 the turnover
2 the profit made after tax
3 the value of the company
4 the cash still available after other investments

Does the company seem to be in a healthy position or not?

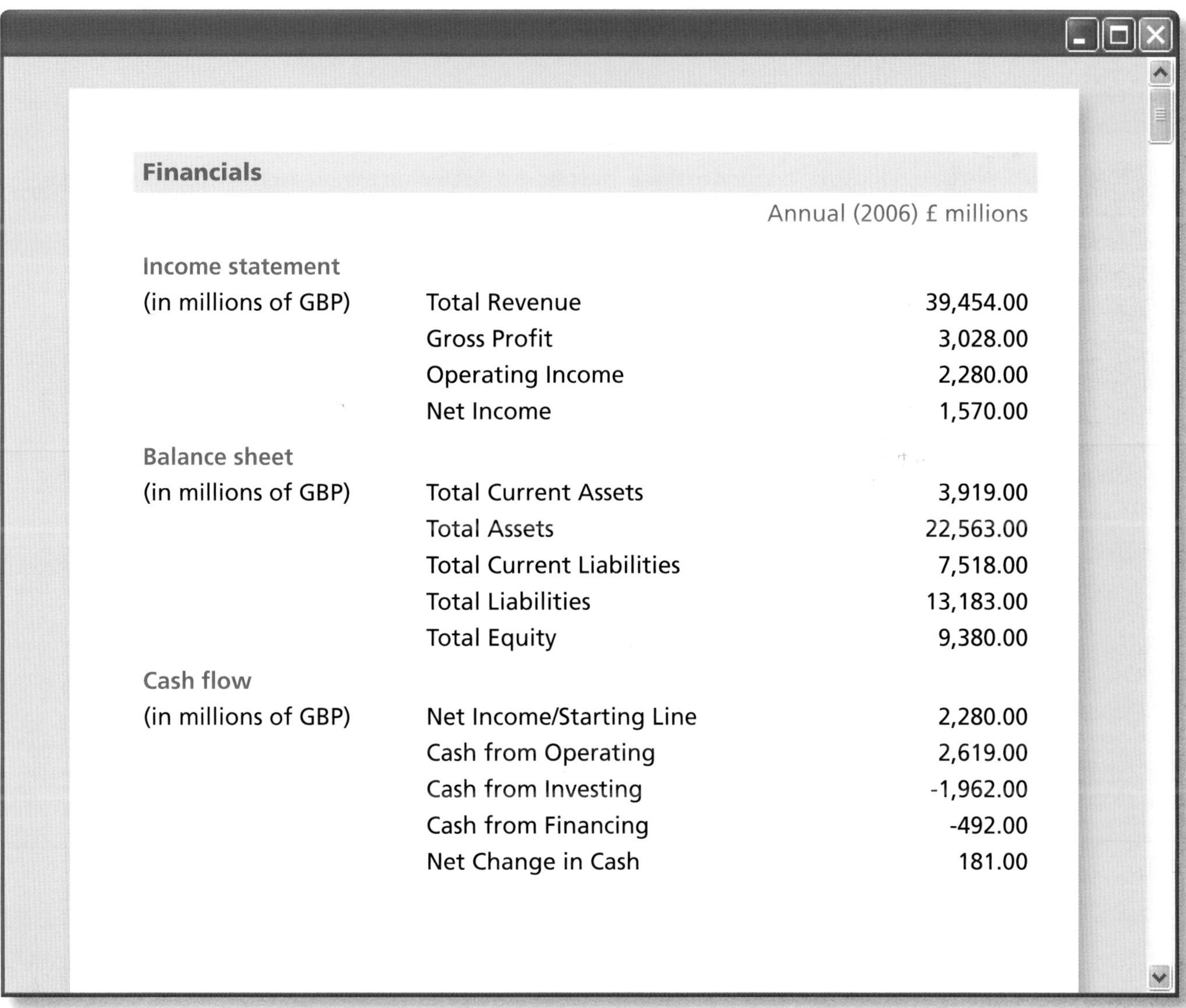

Financials

		Annual (2006) £ millions
Income statement (in millions of GBP)	Total Revenue	39,454.00
	Gross Profit	3,028.00
	Operating Income	2,280.00
	Net Income	1,570.00
Balance sheet (in millions of GBP)	Total Current Assets	3,919.00
	Total Assets	22,563.00
	Total Current Liabilities	7,518.00
	Total Liabilities	13,183.00
	Total Equity	9,380.00
Cash flow (in millions of GBP)	Net Income/Starting Line	2,280.00
	Cash from Operating	2,619.00
	Cash from Investing	-1,962.00
	Cash from Financing	-492.00
	Net Change in Cash	181.00

5.2 Discussing options

VOCABULARY

Business costs

1 Classify these different items in a chocolate manufacturer's costs according to the type of cost.

sugar heating production workers bank charges free samples
vehicle insurance (trucks) ~~lab equipment~~ telephone

1 material costs ____________
2 administrative costs ____________
3 distribution costs ____________
4 overheads ____________
5 labour costs ____________
6 development costs lab equipment
7 advertising expenditure ____________
8 finance costs ____________

LISTENING

Discussing costs

Learning Tip

Look out for these common abbreviations:
lab = laboratory
admin = administrative
gym = gymnasium
ad = advertisement
flu = influenza
sales rep = representative
phone = telephone
fridge = refrigerator
memo = memorandum
PR = public relations
asap = as soon as possible

2 5.2 Listen to this extract from a discussion between a cost accountant and a general manager.

1 Which costs do they discuss?
2 Which cost do they target for making reductions?

3 5.2 Listen again and complete the phrases they use to make and comment on suggestions.

0 OK. What do you suggest?
1 Personally, ____________ cutting the wage bill.
2 No, I ____________ that. ____________ administrative costs or other overheads?
3 ____________ cutting staff, we ____________ try and do something about …
4 ____________, the only real solution is to tackle labour costs.
5 The ____________ of it ____________ be that, once done, we could get back to …
6 OK, ____________ what you're saying, but I think it ____________ create more problems than you think.

SPEAKING

Discussing options and making recommendations

4 **You have an interview for a job with a consulting group that specialises in financial and strategy consulting. At the beginning of your interview they give you this worksheet. Study it and come up with ideas for cost savings.**

For number 1 you could let customers help themselves to napkins, instead of staff handing them out automatically with the burgers. In that way, the company would make a big saving on material costs.

Look at the following companies and think of areas in which cost savings could be made. Remember that reducing advertising or research and development expenditure could damage sales!

1. A well-known hamburger and fast-food chain wants to improve its margins. It has targeted material costs as the simplest area to make savings.
2. A car hire company feels its salary bill is too high and would like to know ways of reducing it without compromising service levels.
3. The market for postal services has recently been opened to competition from other private companies. In this context, the historical Post Office finds that its general operating expenses are too high. It can't increase postage prices because of competition.
4. A German car maker's manufacturing costs are too high, making its cars uncompetitive in the market.
5. A successful clothes and fashion retailing chain wants to reduce the overheads in its stores, which are located in shopping malls and city centres.

Exam Success

Alwayslistencarefully to the contributions of your partner and comment on them. It really helps to promote a natural dialogue, which the examiner will like.

5 **In the interview you are asked to discuss your ideas with another candidate. Work with a partner and exchange ideas. Use the language box to help you.**

Discussing options and making recommendations

So, we've been asked to ... / So, we're here to ...
What do you think / suggest?
What's your opinion / view?
For me, the best thing would be to ...
I'd recommend (doing) ... / We could try (doing) ...
Instead of (doing) ..., we could (do) ...
If we were to (do) ..., then we could (do) ...
The advantage of that would be ...
In that way we would (do) ...
I agree with you.
I think that's an excellent idea.
I see what you're saying, but wouldn't it be better to ...
I think that might be quite difficult / dangerous / expensive ...

5.3 The Listening Test: Part Two

EXAM FORMAT

Part Two of the Listening Test consists of five short monologues on a particular business theme or topic.

The exercise has two parts, each a matching exercise. You will be asked to match each monologue to, for example:

- the identity of the speaker.
- the reason for speaking.
- the topic discussed.
- the attitude of the speaker, etc.

In each case there are eight possibilities to choose from (**A–H**).

The extracts are played once and then repeated a second time.

This is a test mainly of global understanding, but you will also need to pay attention to detail to pick up key information that will lead you to the right choice.

APPROACH

Follow these steps.

- Read the instructions twice and make sure you understand the context of the listening text and what you are being asked to do.
- Look at the focus of each exercise and read the options you are given (**A–H**) for each. The information in the monologues will be contained in some of these options but NOT word for word.
- Some people prefer to do both tasks at once, others to do Task One on the first listening and Task Two on the second listening. Decide which strategy works best for you.
- Put in the answers you are sure of. If there are any gaps at the end, then try to guess the answer.

Exam Success

Remember, you are listening for words and expressions which paraphrase or are synonyms for a word in the answer.

KEY SKILL

Matching

1 5.3 **Listen and read this monologue by a person speaking about the pension crisis. Who is speaking?**

We are accused frequently of doing nothing about the ageing population and the consequent hole in pension funds. But you have to understand that, at the moment at any rate, there are no popular solutions to this problem. Either we raise the retirement age or we increase taxes on working people. Neither of these is a vote winner. I think a lot of us in government are hoping that if we just hold on a bit, then sooner or later another solution will present itself.

2 **Now choose the correct person from the list below. Which phrase(s) led you to the answer?**

TASK ONE – SPEAKER

Match the extract to the correct speaker.

A company director
B politician
C retired employee
D civil servant

3 5.3 **Listen to the extract again. What is his solution? Choose the solution from the list below. What phrase gave you the answer?**

TASK TWO – SOLUTION

Match the extract to the solution proposed.

A to make people retire later
B to increase employees' tax contributions
C to wait until a better idea appears
D to let companies sort it out themselves

EXAM PRACTICE

4 5.4 **Following the approach described above do Practice Test Part Two.**

PART TWO

Questions 1–10

- You will hear five people talking about how they have saved money for their retirement.
- For each extract there are two tasks. For Task One, choose the type of investment each person has made, from the list **A–H**. For Task Two, choose the reason that they give for choosing this pension, from the list **A–H**.
- You will hear the recording twice.

TASK ONE – TYPE OF INVESTMENT

- For questions **1–5** match the extracts with the type of pension or investment each person describes.
- Write one letter **A–H** next to the number of the extract.

1 ....
2 ....
3 ....
4 ....
5 ....

A executive pension plan
B state pension
C company pension scheme
D private pension scheme
E public-sector scheme
F salary-related scheme
G property investment
H high-interest bank account

TASK TWO – REASON

- For questions **6–10** match the extracts with the reasons each speaker gives for the type of investment or pension plan they chose.
- Write one letter **A–H** next to the number of the extract.

6 ....
7 ....
8 ....
9 ....
10 ....

A investment funds haven't performed well
B the government pension is inadequate
C company schemes are safer than private ones
D is very careful with money
E land is expensive and has a poor return
F the welfare state should pay for people's retirement
G the pension scheme is very generous
H the pension is flexible

6.1 Purchasing power

VOCABULARY

Online trading

1 **What does the word *quality* mean to you?**

2 **Read Peter Drucker's definition. Do you agree?**

'Quality in a product or service is not what the supplier puts in. It is what the customer gets out and is willing to pay for. A product is not quality because it is hard to make and costs a lot of money, as manufacturers typically believe. This is incompetence. Customers pay only for what is of use to them and gives them value. Nothing else constitutes quality.'
Peter F. Drucker, Management guru

3 **Do you ever use eBay or a similar online trading place? Why? / Why not?**

4 **These items from an online feedback page describe buyers' and sellers' experiences. Explain what each underlined phrase means.**

0 Item exactly as described. Highly recommended seller.
You should buy from this seller.

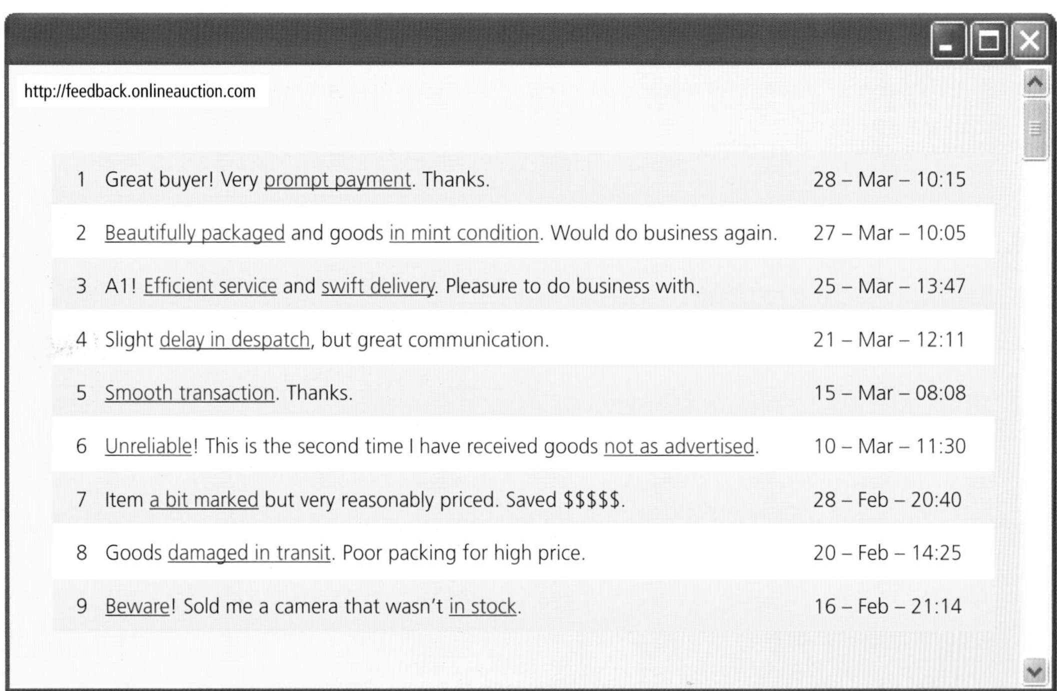

http://feedback.onlineauction.com

1	Great buyer! Very prompt payment. Thanks.	28 – Mar – 10:15
2	Beautifully packaged and goods in mint condition. Would do business again.	27 – Mar – 10:05
3	A1! Efficient service and swift delivery. Pleasure to do business with.	25 – Mar – 13:47
4	Slight delay in despatch, but great communication.	21 – Mar – 12:11
5	Smooth transaction. Thanks.	15 – Mar – 08:08
6	Unreliable! This is the second time I have received goods not as advertised.	10 – Mar – 11:30
7	Item a bit marked but very reasonably priced. Saved $$$$$.	28 – Feb – 20:40
8	Goods damaged in transit. Poor packing for high price.	20 – Feb – 14:25
9	Beware! Sold me a camera that wasn't in stock.	16 – Feb – 21:14

5 **Write feedback for the following two online trading experiences.**

1 John buys some jewellery for a friend's birthday which is in two days' time. The seller promises it will arrive the next day and it does. John writes about the seller.

2 Freda sells a tennis racquet that she bought but never used. The buyer pays immediately, but when it is delivered claims it is second-hand and posts negative feedback. Freda writes about the buyer.

SPEAKING

Managing suppliers

6 **Look at the following supplier–customer pairings. In which case would you expect the relationship to be based on:**

a a close working relationship? b price?

1 a camera manufacturer and an electrical goods retailer
2 a pharmaceutical company and a hospital
3 a haulage (delivery by truck) company and a mail-order clothes retailer
4 a maker of nuts and bolts and a helicopter manufacturer
5 a maker of motors and a helicopter manufacturer

7 **Complete this questionnaire from a business magazine to find out your attitude to suppliers. Compare your answers with your partner.**

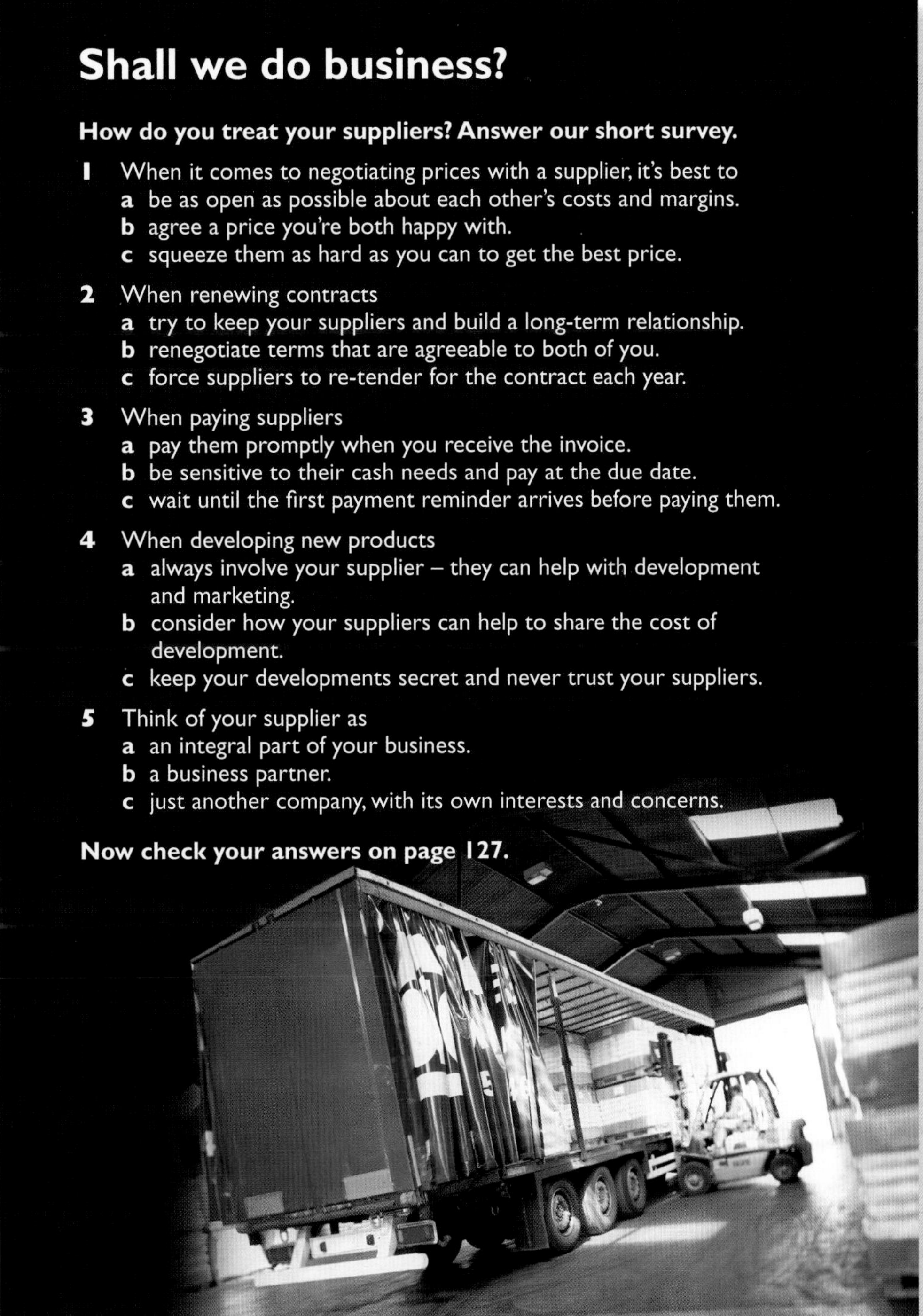

Shall we do business?

How do you treat your suppliers? Answer our short survey.

1 When it comes to negotiating prices with a supplier, it's best to
a be as open as possible about each other's costs and margins.
b agree a price you're both happy with.
c squeeze them as hard as you can to get the best price.

2 When renewing contracts
a try to keep your suppliers and build a long-term relationship.
b renegotiate terms that are agreeable to both of you.
c force suppliers to re-tender for the contract each year.

3 When paying suppliers
a pay them promptly when you receive the invoice.
b be sensitive to their cash needs and pay at the due date.
c wait until the first payment reminder arrives before paying them.

4 When developing new products
a always involve your supplier – they can help with development and marketing.
b consider how your suppliers can help to share the cost of development.
c keep your developments secret and never trust your suppliers.

5 Think of your supplier as
a an integral part of your business.
b a business partner.
c just another company, with its own interests and concerns.

Now check your answers on page 127.

READING

1 Discuss the following questions.

1 How much of your food shopping do you do at supermarkets? Why?
2 Are supermarkets in your country squeezing smaller grocery shops out of the market? Is this a bad thing or a natural development?

2 Read through the text below quickly. What is the problem for suppliers of big supermarkets?

3 Put one word in each space to complete the text.

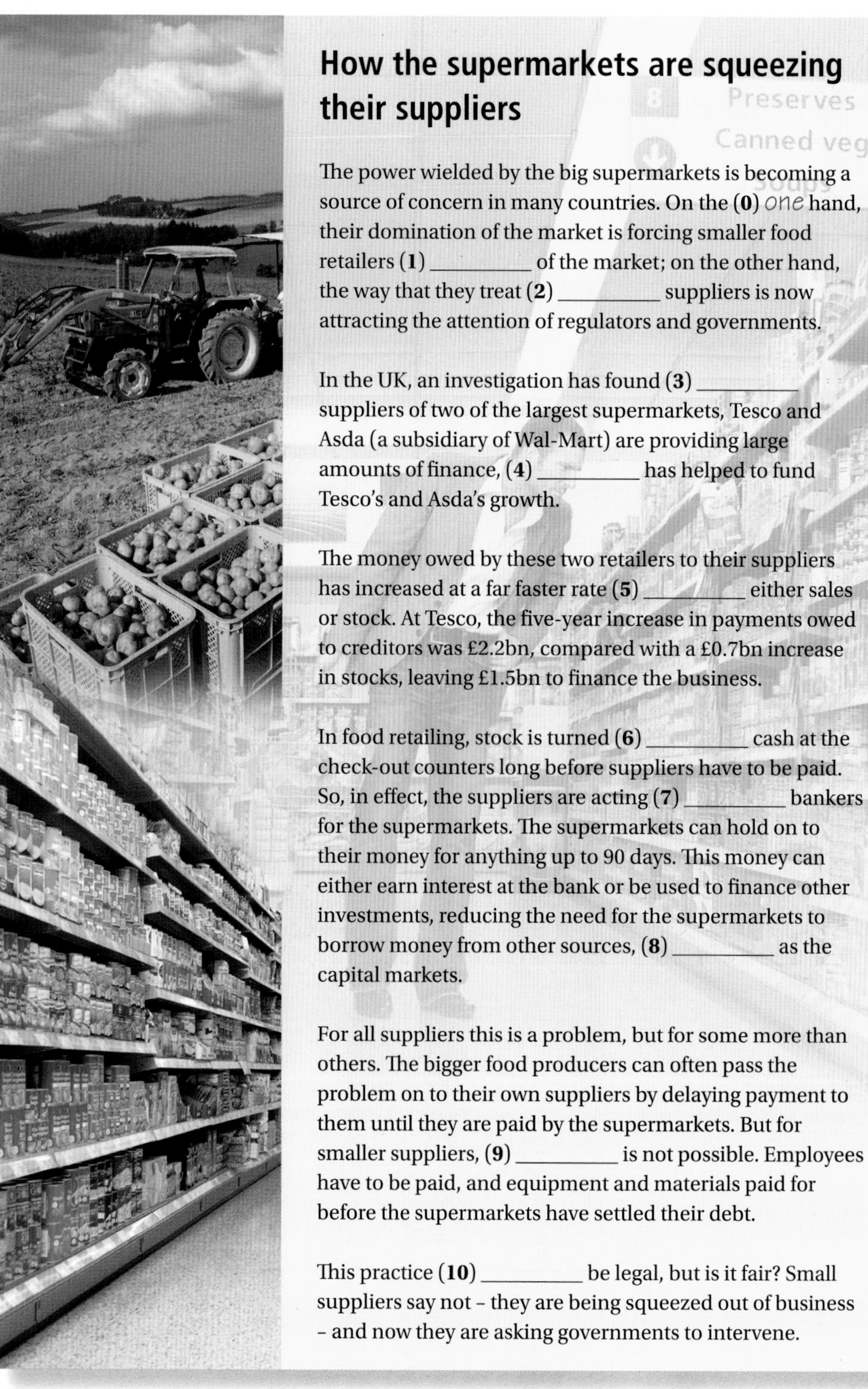

How the supermarkets are squeezing their suppliers

The power wielded by the big supermarkets is becoming a source of concern in many countries. On the **(0)** *one* hand, their domination of the market is forcing smaller food retailers **(1)** _________ of the market; on the other hand, the way that they treat **(2)** _________ suppliers is now attracting the attention of regulators and governments.

In the UK, an investigation has found **(3)** _________ suppliers of two of the largest supermarkets, Tesco and Asda (a subsidiary of Wal-Mart) are providing large amounts of finance, **(4)** _________ has helped to fund Tesco's and Asda's growth.

The money owed by these two retailers to their suppliers has increased at a far faster rate **(5)** _________ either sales or stock. At Tesco, the five-year increase in payments owed to creditors was £2.2bn, compared with a £0.7bn increase in stocks, leaving £1.5bn to finance the business.

In food retailing, stock is turned **(6)** _________ cash at the check-out counters long before suppliers have to be paid. So, in effect, the suppliers are acting **(7)** _________ bankers for the supermarkets. The supermarkets can hold on to their money for anything up to 90 days. This money can either earn interest at the bank or be used to finance other investments, reducing the need for the supermarkets to borrow money from other sources, **(8)** _________ as the capital markets.

For all suppliers this is a problem, but for some more than others. The bigger food producers can often pass the problem on to their own suppliers by delaying payment to them until they are paid by the supermarkets. But for smaller suppliers, **(9)** _________ is not possible. Employees have to be paid, and equipment and materials paid for before the supermarkets have settled their debt.

This practice **(10)** _________ be legal, but is it fair? Small suppliers say not – they are being squeezed out of business – and now they are asking governments to intervene.

Learning Tip

Keep a special notebook for fixed phrases (eg *for the time being*) and phrasal verbs (eg *come across, bring about*) and write example sentences to help memorise them.

4 Do you think suppliers should be protected against the power of big companies? What measures could be taken to do this?

GRAMMAR

Relative and participial clauses

5 **Replace the relative clauses in these sentences with either:**

a an adjective b a present participle (eg *working*) c a past participle (eg *worked*)

0 The money which is owed to suppliers is used to finance other projects.
The money <u>owed</u> to suppliers is used to finance other projects.
1 People who want to use small local shops are unable to do so.
2 The supermarkets which have been accused of unfair competition have denied it.
3 The companies that dominate the market get stronger and stronger.
4 The money which is spent at Tesco accounts for 13% of all UK consumer spending.
5 Suppliers who don't accept these terms are ignored.
6 The goods which customers buy often haven't been paid for by the supermarkets.
7 Suppliers who cannot wait a long time for payment are forced out of the market.

LISTENING

A contract to supply

6 **You have a shop selling flooring products (carpets, tiles, wooden flooring, etc). What would be the most important points to consider when negotiating a contract with your suppliers? Make a list with your partner.**

7 6.1 **Listen to the conversation between Paul (from the retailer, A1 Flooring) and Barbara (from the supplier, Paragon Floors) and choose the correct answer.**

1 Sales of the Klik laminate flooring have been
A poor, even though customers are satisfied with it.
B good, but they could be better.
C good and customer satisfaction is high.

2 In the future, Paul would like to see
A reductions on the products at certain times of year.
B a better commission.
C greater discounts on certain product lines.

3 Barbara doesn't want to
A have a special policy just for A1 flooring.
B give any further discounts.
C mention this to her boss.

4 Another problem for Paul is that
A Paragon's stock levels are too low.
B Paragon can't always supply the precise product ordered.
C Paragon are not flexible enough.

5 Barbara says the shortages of stock are
A due to limited space in their warehouse.
B becoming less of a problem.
C not the fault of Paragon.

6 She says that wood is
A an expensive natural product.
B difficult to store and to move from place to place.
C is available in many different types.

7 Paul says that his customers
A understand the situation.
B will wait for the right product if they have to.
C will take their custom to another retailer.

GRAMMAR

Ordering events: tense practice

1 A woman is having bad experiences with her hot water boiler. These sentences are taken from a letter of complaint she wrote to the manufacturer. Match the two halves of each sentence.

0 In the beginning	A it seemed like the most convenient option.
1 This is the third time that	B I am taking showers at the local swimming pool.
2 On the second occasion	C it was working fine.
3 The next time it breaks down	D I have had to ask for an engineer to come out.
4 At that time	E the engineer never turned up.
5 For the time being	F I am told that my case is very untypical.
6 At no time	G I will take legal action through the small claims court.
7 Every time I call	H I had never had any problems with my boiler.
8 Before that time	I have I tried to repair the boiler myself.

2 Complete this letter by putting the verbs in the correct tense.

Dear Sir

I **(0)** *am writing* (write) to you today because up to now I **(1)** ______________ (be) unable to get a satisfactory answer to my question from your telephone operators. Each time I call the operator **(2)** ______________ (promise) that she will investigate and call me back, but no-one ever does.

Three months ago I purchased a vacuum cleaner from your High Street store in Hertford. At the time it **(3)** ______________ (be) on offer and **(4)** ______________ (seem) like a very good deal. However, on the third occasion that I used it, it **(5)** ______________ (break) down. When I opened it, I discovered that there was a dead mouse in the motor! Since I do not have mice in my home, I concluded that the mouse **(6)** ______________ (get) into the machine before that time, most probably in your factory.

Originally, I intended to ask only for an apology and compensation. However, as this is now the sixth time that I **(7)** ______________ (try) to speak to you about it, I can only assume that you would prefer to discuss the matter in court. Accordingly, the next letter you receive **(8)** ______________ (be) from my lawyer.

I enclose copies of two photographs of the mouse and the vacuum cleaner, which for the time being I **(9)** ______________ (keep) as evidence.

Please be aware that at no time **(10)** ______________ (I / want) to pursue this matter in the courts. It is something you have brought about through your own negligence.

Yours faithfully

Martha Logan

Martha Logan

WRITING

A letter of complaint

3 **The battery on your MP3 player has failed after twelve months of use. Study the following information: an entry from the owner's manual about battery life (A) and a reply from the customer services department to a letter you wrote them asking for a free replacement (B). Do you think this is a satisfactory reply?**

A

We use the best lithium ion battery technology from leading battery manufacturers. The batteries we use are no different than the lithium ion batteries used by any other manufacturer, on products from portable music players, to laptops, to wireless phones. The battery should last most normal users the life of the product (several years).

B

23 January

Dear Mr King

Thank you for your letter of 12 July. Unfortunately, your MP3 player is now out of warranty and we will not be able to replace your battery free of charge. To purchase a new battery please contact our sales team.

Kind regards

Robert Brown
Customer Services

Exam Success

Alwaysmakesurethat you include in your answer all the elements specified in the question. Also think about which elements deserve more attention and which deserve less.

4 **You are not prepared to accept this. Write a letter demanding a free replacement battery. Use this guide to help you.**

Writing guide

- reason for writing (refer to their letter)
- describe the history
- state why you are not satisfied
- suggest next steps
- thank them and close the letter.

26 January

Dear Sir / Madam
I am writing in answer to your letter of 23 January in which you …

6.2 Telephoning

VOCABULARY

Telephone expressions

1 **These are things you commonly hear people say to you on the phone. Respond to them using *will* or *'ll*. Use 2–5 words per space.**

0 Hello, is John there?
Sure, I'll just get him for you.
1 I'm sorry, the line is engaged. Would you like to hold?
No, that's OK. I ________________ later.
2 OK. Can you take a message?
Of course. I ________________ and paper.
3 Can I have the sales department, please?
One moment. I ________________ through.
4 But I need the information by the end of today.
OK, I ________________ as soon as I can.
5 Can you ask Esther to bring her laptop with her?
Sure. I ________________ the message.
6 Is his bill for $3,000 or $3,500?
One second. ________________ my records.
7 Can I speak to Sarah, please?
Hang on. I ________________ back from lunch yet.
8 So, it's the Taj Mahal restaurant at 1 o'clock.
Great. I ________________ to seeing you then.

2 6.2 **Listen and compare your answers.**

SPEAKING

Problems with orders

3 **The following are extracts from telephone conversations between a supplier (a wooden flooring manufacturer, Paragon Floors) and a customer (a flooring retailer, A1 Flooring). Who said what – the customer or the supplier?**

0 'We ordered ten pallets but you only sent us five. I don't know if there's been some misunderstanding.' customer
1 'I'm calling about payment of invoices 2310 and 2324. We sent you a reminder on 4 May, but haven't heard anything. Is there a problem?'
2 'I'm sorry. We don't have that particular item in stock at the moment. Would you accept a replacement of a similar item?'
3 'I received an invoice for the last order (no. 301) but I think we've been overcharged. Can you check it for me?'
4 'I have your order here, but there's no purchase order number on it. Can you send it to me?'
5 'One of the pallets arrived damaged. What's the best thing to do now?'
6 'Delivery was due today, but it's 4 o'clock and I have had no communication, either from you or the delivery firm.'
7 'You're due to receive four pallets of item 501 tomorrow. You may notice that the colour is very slightly different from the one shown in the catalogue. Please check it on arrival and let me know if this is going to be a problem.'

4 **Take the roles of customer and supplier and act out seven telephone conversations. Use the extracts in exercise 3 as the basis for each call. There are some useful phrases in the box below to help you.**

Supplier: One moment, I'll just check. Ah, I can see what happened. We only had five pallets in stock. The others will be with you next week. Is that OK?

Telephoning
Hello. Can I speak to Mr ...? Hello. Can I speak to the person who deals with ...? Hello. I wonder if you can help me. I'm calling about ...?
One moment. I'll put you through. I'll see if he's free.
I'm afraid he's not available. Can I take a message? I'll have to get back to you on that. If you can call me soon, I'd appreciate it.
I'll call back later. Thanks for your help. Thanks for calling. It was nice talking to you.

6.3

Writing Test: Part Two

EXAM FORMAT

Part Two of the Writing Test is a choice between writing a letter, a report or a proposal (200–250 words). Part One carries 10 marks and Part Two 20 marks. Give yourself 40–45 minutes to complete Part Two.

You are expected to respect the conventions and formats of these types of business writing in English. With all types it is most important to answer the question fully. This means addressing all the bullet points in the task.

Reports and proposals

Reports and proposals need to be clearly organised and follow a conventional report / proposal format. They should be divided into paragraphs and have an introduction and conclusion. There is often a paragraph summarising the proposal or (in the case of a report) the findings and they may include a recommendation.

Letter writing

Letters or emails should be divided into clear paragraphs with appropriate opening and closing remarks.

Types of letter include: complaining, explaining and sorting out problems, apologising for a mistake, inviting someone to co-operate in business, etc.

The instructions will describe the situation and list all the elements that you should include in your letter. It may also show an extract of another letter, advertisement, etc to which you have to respond.

Exam Success

Becalmandbusiness-like in your letters: don't make threats or claims you cannot justify; don't exaggerate; and don't be rude.

APPROACH

Letter writing

Follow these steps.

- Read the instructions twice and note all the elements that have to be included in the letter.
- Think carefully about who the letter is for, what your relationship is to the person, and what the reason for writing is. This will determine the *register* (formal, semi-formal, etc) and *tone* (apologetic, determined, etc) of the letter. The tone and the arguments you present must be natural and convincing.
- Plan the letter before beginning to write. You will probably need to include 5–6 paragraphs:
  - introduction
  - reason for writing
  - background to problem
  - possible solutions
  - next steps
  - conclusion.

  By giving it a clear structure you will find it easier to write.
- When you have finished read it back to yourself. Imagine you are the receiver of the letter. Is it clear? Does it sound convincing? Does it achieve its purpose?
- Look for basic grammatical errors (subject-verb agreement, use of tenses, etc).

KEY SKILL

Letter writing conventions

1 **As in any language, letters in English use certain conventions and stock phrases. Below is a list of some of the more common ones. Complete them by adding one word in each space.**

Letter writing conventions

Beginning and ending

Dear Sir / Madam	Yours faithfully
Dear Ms Johnson	Yours (**1**) ________
Dear David	Kind regards

Reason for writing

I am writing to apologise for / enquire about / thank you (**2**) ________ / ...
I am writing (**3**) ________ answer to your letter / enquiry about ...
(**4**) ________ our recent meeting / telephone conversation, I am writing to ...
I was given your name by ..., who suggested you might be able to help us to ...

The background

(**5**) ________ you may know, ... is an ... based in ...
As you will recall, three weeks ago we ...
Recently, we ...

The result

As a result (**6**) ________ this, we have had to ...
Consequently, we would like to ...
The result of this is that ...

The next step

What I propose is that ...
In (**7**) ________ to resolve this matter, I suggest that ...
We would appreciate (**8**) ________ if you could ...
We would be (**9**) ________ if you could now ...

Further communication

Please do not (**10**) ________ to contact me if you wish to discuss any of the above.
I look forward to hearing from you / receiving ...

Signing off

Thank you again for your custom / interest / understanding.
Once (**11**) ________ , my apologies for the delay / misunderstanding / error.
I hope you find this solution satisfactory.

EXAM PRACTICE

2 **Following the approach described above, answer this question from Writing Test Part Two.**

PART TWO

- Write 200–250 words.
- A supplier whom you have dealt with for several years without any problems has recently sent you the wrong stock on three separate occasions.
- Write a **letter** to the company:
  - informing them of the problem
  - explaining the impact it has on your business
  - asking for an explanation for these mistakes
  - suggesting the action you will take if these mistakes continue.

Managing people

Managerial qualities

1 What does this quotation mean?

'A bad manager confuses activity with performance.'

Anon

2 Read this story that was widely circulated on the Internet a few years ago. What does it say about managers that made it so popular?

A man in a hot air balloon realised he was lost. He reduced altitude and spotted a woman below. He descended a bit more and shouted, 'Excuse me, can you help me? I promised a friend I would meet him an hour ago but I don't know where I am.'

The woman below replied, 'You are in a hot air balloon hovering approximately 30 feet above the ground. You are between 40 and 41 degrees north latitude and between 59 and 60 degrees west longitude.'

'You must be an engineer,' said the balloonist.

'I am,' replied the woman. 'How did you know?'

'Well,' answered the balloonist, 'everything you told me is technically correct, but I still have no idea what to make of your information, and the fact is I am still lost. Frankly, you haven't been much help so far.'

The woman below responded, 'You must be in management.'

'I am,' replied the balloonist, 'but how did you know?'

'Well,' said the woman, 'you don't know where you are or where you are going. You have risen to where you are due to a large quantity of hot air. You made a promise, which you have no idea how to keep, and you expect people beneath you to solve your problems. The fact is you are in exactly the same position you were in before we met, but now, somehow, it's my fault.'

3 Number the six most important (1–6) qualities for a manager to possess.

MANAGEMENT MAGAZINE

A good manager is someone who can …

- A delegate responsibility ____
- B plan effectively ____
- C motivate their staff to perform ____
- D handle people sensitively ____
- E organise work efficiently ____
- F recognise and reward good performance ____
- G take tough decisions ____
- H lead by example ____
- I inspire confidence and respect ____
- J communicate their vision and ideas ____
- K co-operate with other parts of the organisation ____
- L be creative and have innovative ideas ____

4 **Discuss your choices with your partner. What are the consequences for the team and the manager if these qualities are absent?**

5 **Look at the list in exercise 3 on page 66 and say what are the key qualities for a *leader* to possess.**

- Are these different from a manager's qualities?
- Is there another leadership quality you would add to the list?

LISTENING

Strengths and weaknesses

6 7.1 **You will hear five employees describing the strengths and weaknesses of their managers.**

- The first time you listen, identify the **weakness** of each manager.
- The second time you listen, identify the **strength** of each manager.

TASK ONE – WEAKNESS

1 ________	A is very disorganised
	B does not co-operate with other departments
2 ________	C does not delegate enough
	D is not good at communicating
3 ________	E does not have clear objectives
	F cannot make quick decisions
4 ________	G is rather insensitive
5 ________	H is not especially clever

TASK TWO – STRENGTH

6 ________	A is a natural communicator
	B challenges his staff to achieve more
7 ________	C is intelligent
	D fits in well in the organisation
8 ________	E has very good people skills
9 ________	F leads by example
	G gives praise and recognition to the team
10 ________	H organises work efficiently

7 **What do you think these phrases from the listening mean?**

1 He's not afraid *to get his hands dirty.*
2 He's a bit of a *control freak.*
3 He *spreads himself very thin.*
4 He often *puts you on the spot.*
5 He doesn't *take on board* what you're saying.
6 She's difficult *to get on with.*
7 She doesn't *have the company's interests at heart.*

VOCABULARY

Idioms: management problems

1 What do you think each of these idioms means?

1 can't see the wood for the trees
2 doesn't want to lose face
3 have tunnel vision
4 bite off more than you can chew
5 too many chiefs, not enough Indians
6 cut corners
7 throw money at the problem
8 open a can of worms
9 be a yes-man

2 Study each of the cases below. Which idiom best fits each case?

0 He had no experience of negotiating. All the same, he volunteered to discuss a settlement to the four-week-old strike with a union leader who had been in the business for 40 years.
He bit off more than he could chew.

1 Asked to find out customer satisfaction rates, the managers at one call centre researched and produced all sorts of data: agent productivity rates, answer delay times, average call times, percentage of problems solved first time, etc.

2 A large electricity supplier is setting up a new customer billing IT system. Four teams are working on the project – the company's IT manager's staff, a software designer, a company in charge of implementing the software and a team of software consultants. After six months very little progress has been made.

3 One of the directors of a bank decides to get tough on people using work phones to make personal calls. This causes a lot of resentment among staff and accusations that managers are just as guilty of this kind of thing as regular staff.

4 Under pressure to reduce costs, a ferry company decided that they could maximise the time their ships were at sea if more safety checks were done while the ships were sailing rather than in the dock.

5 A sales manager had to present her plan for more accurate sales forecasting to the executive board. Two days before her presentation she showed it to a colleague who told her that it had fundamental mistakes in it. So the day before the presentation, she called in sick and asked if the presentation could be postponed to a later date.

6 The government has responded to a lack of hospital beds by building a state of the art, fully-equipped new extension to a city's hospital. Unfortunately, there are not enough trained staff to man it.

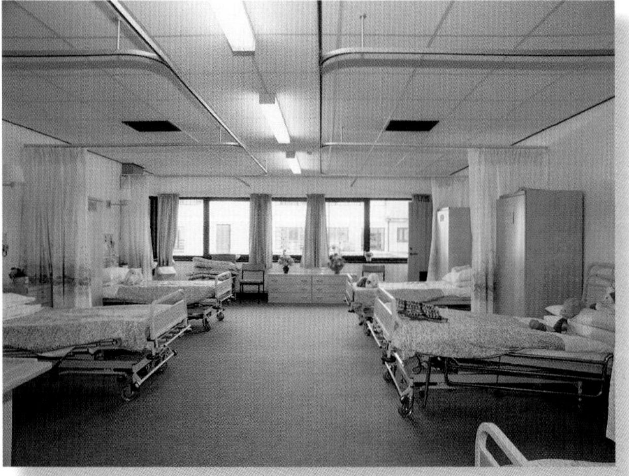

3 What should they have done in each case?

GRAMMAR

Expressing purpose

4 **Read the text from the letters page of *Working Life* magazine and say which of these stress-relieving things you regularly do.**

WORKING LIFE *magazine*

I WAS GETTING REALLY STRESSED and not working efficiently. So I decided to make some simple changes in my working routine. I'd strongly recommend anyone who feels as I did to take time out to think about what they can do to take the stress out of their lives – it's not as difficult as it seems! Here's what I did:

1 made (modest!) lists of what I needed to do each day so that I wouldn't spend my day worrying about what I hadn't done yet.

2 made time for myself to get exercise during the day in order to feel fresher and more able to concentrate when I sat at my desk.

3 learnt to say 'no' to people to avoid taking on more work than I could reasonably handle.

4 spent the first ten minutes of each day in the office reading the news over a coffee just to relax and get my mind working.

5 took time out to stop and chat to colleagues to prevent frustration with a particular task from building up. A good laugh is a great tonic.

5 **Look at the list of actions again and underline the phrases that explain the purpose of each action.**

1 made (modest!) lists of what I needed to do each day so that I wouldn't spend my day worrying.

6 **Make three more sentences describing an action to relieve stress. Explain the precise purpose of each action.**

7 **The CEO of an international clothes retail group felt that his senior managers were not performing as they should. Their skills didn't seem to match the requirements of the business and many seemed to be out of touch with day-to-day operations. So, he devised a seven-point strategy to address the problem.**

- Study the measures. What is the purpose of each measure?
- Write a sentence explaining the purpose of each one, using the phrases from exercise 4.

1 They need to undergo an assessment ***in order to find out*** where their real strengths and weaknesses are.

From 1 January next year all senior managers will:

1 undergo an assessment of their skills by an external management consultant.

2 be set clear, concrete and practical targets for the year.

3 spend at least one day per month working at a high street retail store.

4 spend at least three months every three years in an overseas subsidiary.

5 participate in team-building activities once a year with their team.

6 devote at least six hours per month to foreign language training.

7 follow at least one course per year in communications skills (managing meetings, negotiating, etc).

READING

Management consultants

1 **What do you think of management consultants? Do they have a good or bad reputation in your country (or company)?**

Exam Success

If you don't know the answer immediately, try to eliminate some of the options. Perhaps a word doesn't fit grammatically, or perhaps the sense seems wrong.

2 **Read the letter from a management consultant defending his profession. Choose the best word (A, B, C or D) to fill each gap.**

Dear Editor

Your article on 5 September 'Consultants – who needs them?' gives a very one-sided view of our profession.

We consultants are often criticised for using management buzzwords to sell our services. The critics' **(1)**______ is that we dress up an old concept and present it to companies as a revolutionary idea that will **(2)**______ their business. So when we encourage companies to 'analyse their value chain', we are saying nothing more than 'see which part of the business is most profitable'. When we **(3)**______ them to 'empower their employees', we are just saying **(4)**______ them to do a good job. The terms we use, the critics say, is just jargon for things that all businesses know they have to do anyway.

We're also accused **(5)**______ hypocrisy. The classic example of this is when during the 1990s consultancy firms told companies to concentrate on their core competencies and outsource non-essential activities to contractors who could do a better and cheaper job. But, the critics scream, you **(6)**______ a lot of the early 1980s telling companies to diversify and get involved in new businesses.

Maybe we are sometimes guilty of following the **(7)**______ trends in management, but I have one **(8)**______ simple answer for the critics. Knowing the need for these management concepts and practices is one thing; actually using them and **(9)**______ them is another. Our job is to remind businesses to do the things they ought to be doing. That is the role of consultants and it's a very **(10)**______ role. We're not saying managers are stupid, but just that it's human nature sometimes to ignore the obvious.

John Birdman
(Partner – Salix Associates)

	A	B	C	D
1	A theme	B argument	C speech	D debate
2	A transform	B modify	C transfigure	D reverse
3	A explain	B say	C force	D urge
4	A entrust	B believe	C trust	D involve
5	A by	B of	C on	D with
6	A lasted	B took	C passed	D spent
7	A last	B latest	C freshest	D least
8	A absolutely	B completely	C very	D utterly
9	A implementing	B effecting	C realising	D installing
10	A hopeful	B thoughtful	C useful	D careful

Do you agree with him?

GRAMMAR

Word order: adverbs

3 **Study these basic rules of word order in English.**

Word order: adverbs

1 Don't separate a verb from its direct object.
He left ~~early~~ the party *early*.
2 Adverbs generally go after the main verb.
She drove *carefully*.
3 Adverbs of frequency (*often, always,* etc) and qualifiers (*really, absolutely,* etc) go before the main verb.
They *always* bring a gift of some kind.
I *really* like him.
4 With *be*, adverbs of frequency go after the verb.
He is *always* in meetings when I call.
5 Phrases expressing time (*in the morning, three days ago, last year,* etc) can go at the beginning or the end of a sentence.
***Last year* I didn't have a summer holiday.**
I didn't have a summer holiday *last year*.
6 We usually put place before time.
I've lived *in Oxford for ten years*

4 **Put the word / phrase in brackets into the correct place in each sentence.**

0 I didn't arrive at his house. (until after 8 o'clock).
I didn't arrive at his house until after 8 o'clock.
1 Don't worry. I can catch the bus. (easily)
2 I intended to stay in this job for so long. (never)
3 She goes back to her house each weekend. (in the country)
4 I like Cate Blanchett's films. (a lot)
5 All my troubles seemed so far away. (yesterday)
6 It will take a long time to get an answer from them. (probably)
7 He fell in love with Los Angeles the day he arrived. (hopelessly)
8 She was amazed at the progress we had made. (absolutely)
9 It is quite difficult to persuade someone to buy on the spot. (often)
10 They attended the conference in London. (last week)

5 **Correct the word order in these statements about management.**

0 I try usually to delegate responsibility to my team.
I usually try to delegate responsibility to my team.
1 She handles very sensitively the problems.
2 She reads in the morning all her emails on the train to work.
3 In his office he holds a team meeting every Monday.
4 She leads always by example.
5 Her staff very much like her.

7.2 Report writing

WRITING

A business report

1 This quotation could apply to any kind of business writing. What does it mean to you?

'I have made this letter longer than usual, only because I have not had the time to make it shorter.'

Blaise Pascal (French Mathematician)

2 Apart from conciseness, what are the other ingredients of a good business report? Work with a partner and make a list.

3 The business report below was written in response to the following request. Make a note of the report's good points and bad points.

Request

Hi Davina

John is asking me for a progress report on the documentary film about Greenland.

Can you please send me a formal report outlining:

- the reasons for making this documentary
- how far you have got with the project
- any problems experienced
- the schedule from now up to completion

Thanks

Paula

Report

Progress report on Greenland documentary

This is just to bring you up to date on the documentary we started last May, to let you know what we have so far and when we expect to be finished.

We decided to make a documentary about Greenland because first, no-one else is doing one at the moment and secondly, because it's a good place to see the effects of global warming, which we all know is a topical subject just now.

We've shot about five hours of material and have some great shots of wildlife – especially polar bears – and some really interesting interviews with local people.

It's taken a bit longer than expected because the weather is kind of unpredictable and we've spent quite a lot of time waiting around for it to change. Another problem has been getting permissions to shoot up in the north. It's a conservation area and the authorities have been pretty tight about letting us film.

We reckon that we only have another four weeks filming to do and then it's back to the editing room to try to distil it all down to only an hour.

One thing that we're not really sure about is the angle that you'd like to take on this. Is it just a wildlife film? Should it be about global warming? Should it focus more on the people? It'd be nice to have your views on this before we get to the cutting room.

4 Rewrite the report, improving it in the ways you have agreed.

VOCABULARY

Linking phrases

5 **Linking ideas is an important part of report writing. Rewrite each sentence using the words or phrases to give the same meaning.**

1 He's rich, *but* he's unhappy.
  0 Although he's rich, he's unhappy.
  a In spite of / Despite ______________________ .
  b ______________________ . Nevertheless ______________________ .

2 It's complex *and* expensive.
  a In addition to ______________________ .
  b As well as ______________________ .
  c ______________________ . Furthermore ______________________ .

3 They will produce a report *when* they have gathered all the evidence.
  a After ______________________ .
  b ______________________ . Subsequently, ______________________ .

4 The company went bankrupt *because* it was poorly managed.
  a ______________________ on account of ______________________ .
  b ______________________ . Consequently, ______________________ .

WRITING

A report on employee training

Exam Success

Always read your finished piece of writing back to yourself. First check it flows logically. Then look for errors with tenses, subject–verb agreement and spellings.

6 **Solartech is a company that makes solar panels. Demand for this technology is growing fast and in the last two years the company has employed twenty new people in the sales department. The company is concerned that these new recruits either lack sales experience or do not have a good technical understanding of the product. It would like a report on this situation as soon as possible.**

Write a report describing:

- the scope of your survey.
- how many new recruits are not performing well and what their problems are.
- any positive findings.
- recommendations for remedying the situation.

7.3 Reading Test: Part Two

EXAM FORMAT

Part Two of the Reading Test consists of a text 400–500 words long, commenting on some aspect of business or working life. The passage will be taken from a newspaper, business magazine, management guide or company report.

The exercise involves fitting missing sentences (from a choice of eight) into six gaps in the text. It requires you to understand how sentences in a text are linked to each other in meaning and structure. Give yourself 10–12 minutes to complete the task.

APPROACH

Follow these steps.

- Read the instructions twice and make sure you understand the context of the passage and what you are being asked to do.
- Read the passage through quickly (two minutes). What is the subject? What is the main argument?
- Re-read the passage to the first gap and study carefully the sentences before and after the gap. What information do you expect to be included here?
- Find the sentence from the list (**A–H**) that best fits.
- Repeat this process for the other gaps.
- Read the whole text (with the gaps filled) back to yourself quickly to make sure it makes sense.

KEY SKILL

Cohesion

Exam Success

Practisethisexercise by choosing a sentence in a text at random and asking yourself how it relates to the passage as a whole and particularly the sentences around it, both grammatically and in meaning.

1 **Look at this passage. Predict what kind of information the missing sentence is likely to contain.**

According to legend, inventors have frequently come up with designs for an everlasting light bulb. These products would cost no more to make. But a conspiracy of light bulb manufacturers has always ensured that these innovations are suppressed, so that the continuing market for light bulbs is not spoiled. The product is not always a light bulb. (**1**) _____ And why don't batteries go on forever? It must surely be possible to build automobiles that would never wear out.

2 **Look at the options. Which one is correct? Does it correspond to your prediction?**

A The same claims are made for tights: what woman would not rush to purchase a pair of long-lasting tights?
B Light bulbs typically last between 1,000 and 1,500 hours.
C The truth is that it is not in company's interests to make products which last.

3 **What kind of information is this missing sentence likely to contain?**

One dictionary defines innovation as the introduction of something new or different. (**2**) _____ What it can do is propel you ahead of the competition, restructure an industry or shift customer perceptions. Perhaps six years ago we too were guilty of putting innovation in a box, seeing it as the preserve of only those employees who worked in research and development, or perhaps marketing.

4 **Look at the options. Which is correct? Why?**

A In the UK, for example, it has now become part of a company's culture.
B These employees must embrace it as something which is critical to success.
C That's a fairly boring description of a concept so full of promises.

EXAM PRACTICE **5** **Following the approach described above do Practice Test Part Two.**

PART TWO

Questions 1–6.

- Read this text about VW's new corporate university.
- Choose the best sentence **A–H** to fill each of the gaps **1–6**.
- Do not use any letter more than once.
- There is an example at the beginning (**0**)

Corporate universities

Internationally, there is a trend towards corporate universities. More and more companies feel that the education system, and state universities in particular, are not meeting the needs of industry and big business. (**0**) ...C..... The concept originated in the US, where 1,600 such institutions are now owned by private companies. The number of corporate universities has quadrupled in the last fifteen years. In six years, it is estimated, more people worldwide will attend corporate than state universities.

But some education experts point to the poor performance and very limited scope of subjects in many corporate universities. (**1**) ....

Some go even further, accusing companies who establish corporate universities of trying to mould their employees to be perfect corporate citizens. (**2**) ....

At VW, the German car manufacturer, which has recently announced the building of a new corporate university, they are aware of these criticisms. (**3**) .... The company, in all modesty, calls their new Car Uni 'the prototype of a new corporate university'. So what is it that it will do differently?

The main difference between the VW and some other corporate universities is that the Car Uni aspires to become something like a 'proper university'. Future students can earn two degrees here: an MA in global leadership, and an MSc in organisational excellence. (**4**) .... A different order from, say, McDonald's corporate Hamburger University, where sellers of chips can become 'restaurant assistant managers'.

The Car Uni will consist of three schools – economics and business administration, sciences and technology, and human and social sciences – an impressively broad scope of subjects compared with other corporate universities. (**5**) ....

The Car Uni is an ambitious project indeed. But not everyone is impressed. Swiss scholar Peter Glotz, who researches the effectiveness of different education systems and has also studied corporate universities, warns that VW might be on the wrong track. (**6**) .... 'Companies must develop platforms with which they can make use of the universities of the world, not build academies of their own.'

A They say they would like to avoid the typical mistakes of corporate universities.

B According to him, building a big campus and, especially, employing a lot of staff are completely unnecessary.

C Instead they prefer to train their staff in a specific way.

D He suggests that corporate university graduates will not be equipped to work anywhere outside the company.

E Moreover, it will open its doors to postgraduates in 2009, even if they are not employed by VW.

F They claim that these so-called universities offer little more than job training for their employees and lack a scientific foundation in research.

G Both will be certified and accredited.

H In other words, to produce 'graduates' who are not only equipped with the right skills, but who also never deviate from the company philosophy.

8.1 Being responsible

VOCABULARY

Environmental problems

Kermit the Frog

1 **In which of the following areas are you environmentally conscious? What things do you do which are not so environmentally friendly? Give examples.**

Action with impact on the environment	Friendly	Less friendly
1 saving energy	I use low-energy light bulbs.	
2 using public transport		
3 limiting how much you fly		
4 conserving water		
5 recycling waste		
6 purchasing green products		
7 supporting local shops and businesses		

2 **Which of these environmental problems:**

a are natural?
b are man-made?
c could be either?

earthquakes oil spills at sea nuclear radiation leaks hurricanes landslides smog declining fish stocks drought extinction of different species flooding chemical explosions volcanic eruptions

3 **Which of these problems has your country experienced in recent years? How were they handled? What precautions have been taken against future occurrences?**

READING

4 **Of these three groups in society, who can do most to combat pollution and climate change?**

a individual consumers
b large companies
c governments

5 **Below is an extract from *The Little Earth Book* suggesting a possible way to control man-made pollution. Read the text quickly. Which of these sentences do you think the author would agree with?**

a Americans pollute more because they produce more of the world's wealth.
b The USA's pursuit of wealth is damaging the planet for everyone else.
c There are more important problems than damage to the environment.
d Damage to the environment is the most important problem in the world today.
e We can solve the problem if we all do something to help in our own lives.
f This problem requires concerted action from governments and international organisations.

Trading pollution quotas

How can we eliminate pollution? The biggest threat the world has ever faced is the rising level of greenhouse gases in the atmosphere. We must reduce emissions to a level that the world can sustain. There is no alternative. These gases are an essential part of a balanced ecosystem; it is only in excess that they become dangerous. But to get them back to a safe level, emissions will have to be reduced by over 60%. Since financial markets are so powerful, they should be designed to reward countries for reducing emissions. A mechanism for doing this is quite simple and obvious, and is only obscured by industrial countries attempting to avoid paying a fair price for their resources. Here is how such a market could operate.

- On average everyone in the world is responsible for 4.21 tonnes of carbon emissions a year.
- If the atmosphere can only sustain a limited quantity of carbon dioxide, should one person be allowed to emit a lot more than another? Everyone should have an equal allowance, ie 4.21 tonnes at present, but reducing with time.
- An Indian emits 0.81 tonnes on average and therefore has a surplus of 3.4 tonnes available for sale.
- An average American emits 19.53 tonnes. He therefore needs to buy 15.32 tonnes in order to maintain his lifestyle.

Multiplied by population this means that India has 3.2 billion tonnes of CO_2 for sale and the US needs to buy 4.1 billion tonnes. The US needs to buy the whole of India's surplus and more besides. Alternatively the US must reduce its emissions. Trading on this basis means that money would flow from the rich nations, which are causing the climate havoc, to poor nations that are suffering from it. The UN development programme commented, 'such flows would be neither aid nor charity. They would be the outcome of a free-market mechanism that penalises the richer nations' over-consumption of the global commons.' Thus a fair market system for tradable quotas would result in a fairer world. Each nation's allowance could then gradually be reduced on an equal per capita basis to a globally sustainable level.

6 **Underline the sentences in the text that support your answer to exercise 5 above. Compare your answers with a partner.**

7 **Which of the sentences in exercise 5 above do you agree with?**

8 **Do you think such a trading system would work? Why? / Why not?**

9 **How do you pronounce the following figures?**

1 60% 2 4.21 tonnes per year 3 3.2bn tonnes of CO_2

READING

Learning Tip

If a subject interests you, read around it as much as you can. www.bbc.co.uk is an excellent website for news and ideas on a huge range of topics.

1 **Read the conclusion to the passage 'Trading pollution quotas' below. In most lines there is an extra word that is unnecessary or grammatically incorrect. But some lines are correct.**

- If there is an extra word write the word in the margin.
- If there is no extra word in the line write CORRECT in the margin.

TRADING POLLUTION QUOTAS

0	Not practical? Rich nations may not like it the thought of inhabiting a fair	IT
00	and equitable world, but multi-nationals might not object – if a millionaire	CORRECT
1	becomes being a billionaire he is not going to drink any more Coca Cola, but	
2	an Indian rising out of poverty becomes a marketing opportunity. But that's	
3	another story – and perhaps another clutch of problems. What are there the	
4	alternatives? Regions that they suffer catastrophic loss due to pollution by	
5	the rich nations should have a case in international law. If so, their claim for	
6	damages would be considerably more greater than the 'Third World Debt'.	

GRAMMAR

Use of prepositions with statistics

2 **Choose the best preposition to complete each sentence.**

1. *At / On* average, an Indian emits 0.81 tonnes of carbon per year.
2. Emissions will have to be reduced *for / by* 60% to get them back to a safe level.
3. Three *out of / from* ten of the world's cars are driven by Americans, producing half the world's exhaust fumes.
4. *Over / Through* the last 30 years we have seen a rise *in / of* global temperatures *by / of* more than 1°C.
5. The UK has set a target of maintaining its emissions *with / at* 1990 levels.
6. *By / On* the end of the century sea levels will rise *between / from* two and four metres.

3 **These statements are from a US scientist who thinks the environmentalists are exaggerating. Complete them by putting one preposition in each space.**

1. The number of bald eagles has risen ________ 1500% since 1965.
2. Air pollution fell in America last year ________ the lowest level ever recorded.
3. US forests expanded ________ 9.5 million acres ________ 1990 and 2000.
4. Wetland areas have also increased ________ the last five years.
5. There will be a decline ________ emissions from cars ________ 80% in the next 30 years.
6. Fish stocks have stabilised ________ their 1995 levels.
7. Two ________ ________ three of the targets set by the Clean Air Act have been reached.
8. ________ average, Americans now cause less pollution than five years ago.

4 **Look at the graph describing the disposal of waste in the USA between 1970 and the present. Write five more sentences about the facts it shows using the prepositions on page 78.**

Since 1970, the total amount of waste produced in the USA has increased by almost 300%.

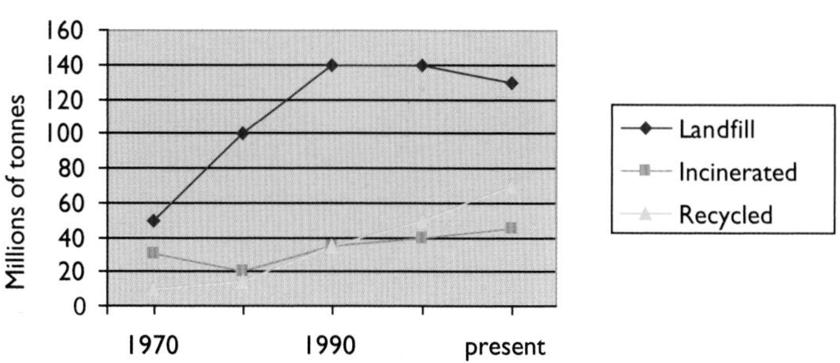

WRITING

Describing a graph

5 **The two graphs below show global temperature changes and carbon dioxide emissions from 1880 to 1990. Study the graphs and discuss with your partner the developments in each and the relationship between the two. Is there a connection?**

- Using information given in the graphs, write a short report (120–140 words) describing these changes and the possible connections between them.
- Begin like this:

The graphs show the changes in global temperatures and the amount of carbon dioxide emitted by different countries over the period 1880 to 1990. Taking global temperature first, we can see that …

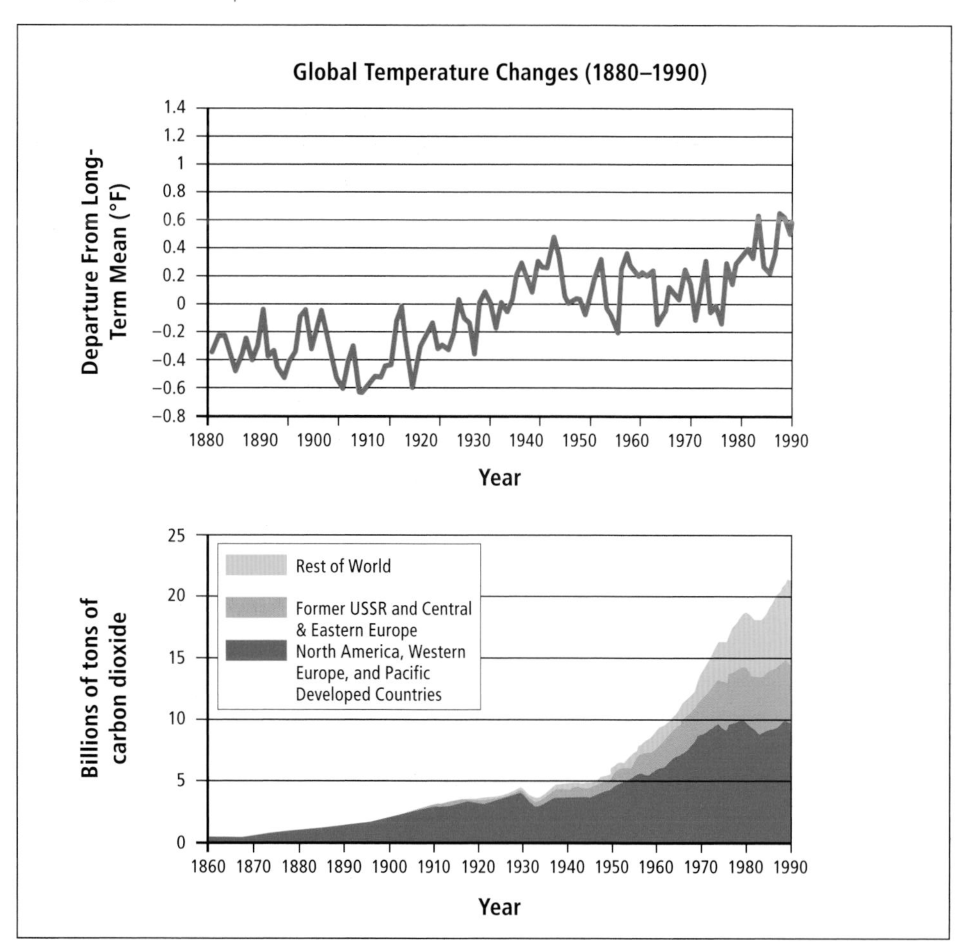

Corporate social responsibility

1 **Stakeholders are all those people who play a part in or are affected by a company's activities. Which group(s) of stakeholder are most affected in each of these cases?**

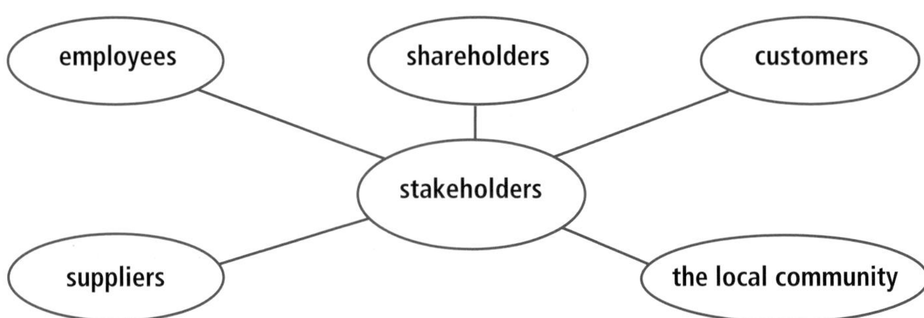

1 An oil company overstates its profits in its half-yearly financial report.
2 A big supermarket decides to label the salt and sugar content in all its foods.
3 A manufacturer of washing machines sets up a recycling scheme to take old washing machines back at the end of their useful lives.
4 A brewer and distributor of beer makes a TV advertisement that children find very funny.
5 A high street bank lays off 350 permanent staff and re-employs 200 of them on temporary contracts.
6 An electronics retailer increases its payment terms to trade creditors from 30 to 60 days.

2 8.1 **You will hear the CEO of a company talk about a particular approach to corporate social responsibility. As you listen, complete the notes to the talk. You can use up to three words per space.**

CORPORATE SOCIAL RESPONSIBILITY

The theory

1 The new concept is called ______________________.
2 The three areas in which to measure a company's performance are financial, social and ______________________.
3 These three legs are ______________________.

The reasoning behind it

4 People's lives are affected more by business than by ______________________.
5 The environment is under great ______________________.
6 Business can play a part in ______________________.
7 Businesses don't always take into account the impact of their actions ______________________.

The practice

8 To make a difference companies have to ______________________.
9 They must recognise their responsibilities to all their ______________________.
10 They must also submit to financial, environmental and social ______________________.
11 Companies have to be honest and open about ______________________.
12 It's not easy for a private company to disclose their ______________________.

Can this approach work? What could be the disadvantages of it?

Gerunds and infinitives

3 **Gerunds and infinitives**

Some words and expressions in English are followed by the gerund (*-ing*) and some are followed by the infinitive (*to*).

In this example from the listening on page 80, the word *committed* is followed by the preposition *to* and the gerund.
They must also be committed to respecting their employees.

In this other example from the listening on page 80, the phrase *It's not enough* is followed by the infinitive.
It's not enough to say you are going to follow a policy.

4 **Look at these English sayings. Put the verb in the correct form: gerund (*-ing*) or infinitive (*to ...*)**

1 It takes all sorts ________ (make) a world.
2 You can't make an omelette without ________ (break) eggs.
3 It's no use ________ (cry) over spilt milk.
4 If a job's worth _____ (do), it's worth ________ (do) well.
5 It's better ________ (be) safe than sorry.
6 It's easy ________ (be) wise after the event.
7 Before ________ (criticise) a man, walk a mile in his shoes.
8 It's never too late ________ (learn).
9 You have to be able ________ (walk) before you can run.
10 If you are in a hole, stop ________ (dig).

5 **What does each saying mean? Do you have an equivalent proverb in your own language?**

6 **Choose two of the proverbs above. Think of situations from your own experience which you could apply each one to. Describe the situations to your partner. See if they can guess which proverb is applicable to each.**

I got very angry with my boss recently because he wouldn't make a decision about employing extra staff, who we really needed to help get a project finished. I thought he was just being indecisive, but then he told me that Head Office had cut his budget by one third. I felt really embarrassed.

7 **Complete these sentences (all the expressions take the same grammatical form).**

1 Our company is committed ____________________.
2 If you visit my country, you will have to get used ____________________.
3 I am really looking forward ____________________.
4 I don't mind paying, but I do object ____________________.

Formal meetings

VOCABULARY

Business meetings

1 The phrases in bold are taken from a business meeting. What do they mean?

1 So, what's **on the agenda** for today?
2 Is anyone **taking the minutes**?
3 I think we should **adjourn** for lunch.
4 Who's supposed to be **chairing** this meeting?
5 Can I just **sum up** the main points we've agreed?
6 Sorry, can I just **butt in** for a moment?
7 We're running short of time. Can we **move on**?
8 I think Jade is **better placed** to answer than me.

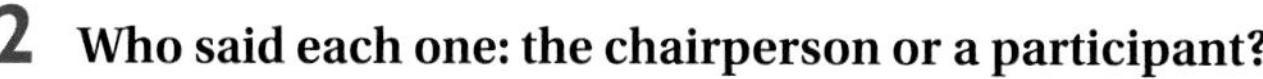

2 Who said each one: the chairperson or a participant?

GRAMMAR

Modal verbs

3 Look at the sentences taken from a company's ethics code. What obligation is placed on the employee in each case? Match each modal verb in bold to an adjective (A–E).

A compulsory
B advisable (a good idea)
C permitted
D unnecessary
E forbidden

1 You **may** take an outside job, if there is no conflict of interest.
2 You **should** at all times act in the best interests of the company.
3 If you give or receive a gift whose value is under $40 you **don't have to** declare it.
4 You **mustn't** use knowledge you have about the company which is not public to speculate with its shares.
5 All company assets, even stationery, **must** be used for company business, not personal gain.
6 You **should** always represent the services of the company to the customer as honestly and openly as possible.
7 You **must not** pass on classified information, such as customer data, to any third party.

4 Imagine an employee broke the code. Which rules in exercise 3 do these crimes or offences relate to?

bribery insider dealing breach of confidence theft misselling

SPEAKING

Discussing business ethics

5 **What does the term *whistleblowing* mean? You are going to agree a policy for your company. Read the information below.**

Your company, a national newspaper, has already defined a code of business ethics covering such things as payments given for information, confidentiality, receipt of gifts, etc.

Its next task is to define a policy on 'internal whistleblowing': in other words what happens when one employee would like to alert the company to the unethical practice of another employee.

You are going to meet with your colleagues to discuss and agree this policy.

6 **Before you meet, the following list is circulated among you. Look at the sentences below and choose the modal verb that indicates what you think is the correct policy.**

1 If you become aware that another employee has broken the ethical code you *must / may / don't have to* report it.
2 When reporting such breaches you *must / don't have to / mustn't* give your name.
3 If you only suspect unethical practice, but cannot prove it, you *must / should / mustn't* report it.
4 The management *must / may / doesn't have to* treat any accusations of unethical practice in confidence.
5 The accused *should / doesn't have to / mustn't* know the identity of his or her accuser.
6 The whistleblower s*hould / may / mustn't* benefit personally from his action by way of promotion or other personal gain.

7 **Look at the agenda and prepare for the meeting. Nominate one person to chair the meeting. (The chairperson may find the phrases at the bottom of the page useful.)**

Agenda

1 Whistleblowing – a right or a duty?
2 The right to anonymity
3 Rewards for whistleblowers
4 Any other business

Chairing a meeting

OK. Shall we start?
As you know, we're here to discuss / talk about / consider ...
The aim of this meeting is to ...
Carlos, would you like to begin?
I think we should move on to the next point.
Perhaps we can come back to this later.
Can I just interrupt you, Carlos?

So, to sum up, we've agreed that ...
Does anyone have anything further to add?
OK. Let's leave it there. Thank you all for your input.

8.3 Reading Test: Part Four

EXAM FORMAT

Part Four of the Reading Test consists of a business text approximately 250 words long. It is a gapped text, with ten single words missing. The exercise involves choosing one of four words to fill each gap. It tests your knowledge of vocabulary and grammar.

Give yourself ten minutes to complete the task.

APPROACH

Follow these steps.

- Read the instructions twice and make sure you understand the context of the passage and what you are being asked to do.
- Read the passage through quickly (two minutes) to get the general meaning.
- Re-read the passage to the first gap and look at the whole sentence. What word would fit grammatically and in meaning?
- Look at the choices and choose the one that fits best. Look out especially for what comes directly after the gap: a particular preposition, an infinitive or gerund, etc.
- If you cannot decide, eliminate the ones that definitely don't fit.
- Repeat this process for the other gaps.

KEY SKILL

Choosing the right word

1 Look at this sentence. Think of a word that fits the gap. Is your word one of the four words below?

In order to _______ in negotiating a good deal, the first thing to understand is the position of your negotiating partner.

A accomplish B win C succeed D thrive

Note: *succeed* is the only one that fits because it takes the proposition *in* after it (*win* and *thrive* take *at*, *accomplish* is followed by a noun).

2 Choose a word for these sentences. Explain why you chose this word.

1 But if job opportunities exist, how do we _______ for the large number of unemployed people?
A explain B account C justify D claim

2 So companies must be _______ responsible for cleaning up the waste that they create.
A taken B kept C had D held

3 Producing chemicals on such a large _______ the company has attracted the attention of many environmental groups.
A scale B extent C degree D size

Exam Success

Askyourteacherfor exercises in 'collocation' – words which naturally go together, eg *take measures, fierce competition*, etc

EXAM PRACTICE **3** **Following the approach described on page 84 do Practice Test Part Four.**

PART FOUR

Questions 1–10

- Read this article about recycling.
- Choose the correct word (**A**, **B**, **C** or **D**) to fill each gap.
- There is an example at the beginning (**0**).

GREEN DREAM

Your home is full of recycling bins and your cupboards are filled with food (**0**) ……… in fairtrade and organic labels. You're careful to turn off the lights whenever you leave a room and wouldn't dream of leaving the TV on (**1**) ……… . On the domestic front, you're as green as (**2**) ……… be.

But at work it's a different story. All that wasted paper, the unfairly traded tea and coffee, the lights left on overnight, the computers blazing out heat all day (**3**) ……… . Although many businesses are getting serious about sustainability, some still (**4**) ……… to provide recycling bins or to consider the environmental impacts of their products and services. If your employer is one of those who hasn't yet gone green, how can you make them change their (**5**) ………?

The first thing is to talk to your boss. (**6**) ……… on the bottom line. Talk about the risks your company faces. Climate change: what impact will it have on profits? Rising oil prices: how are you going to manage the costs? Limits on the (**7**) ……… of CO_2: what will they mean for your business? Remind your boss that managing these risks can save the business money.

Then go in for the kill. The risks are an issue, but they're not (**8**) ……… as important as the opportunities. The next thing for business is to be the biggest and best at meeting the growing demand for solutions to these problems. Just look at the success of fairtrade coffee. And the Toyota Prius. You and your boss could come (**9**) ……… with the next great idea.

Any company that can develop (**10**) ……… products and services that address wider environmental or societal problems is going to do well.

Example:

	A	B	C	D
0	**A** plastered	**B** stuck	(**C**) covered	**D** surrounded

	A	B	C	D
1	**A** reserve	**B** standby	**C** backup	**D** shutdown
2	**A** can	**B** should	**C** might	**D** will
3	**A** through	**B** over	**C** out	**D** long
4	**A** fail	**B** manage	**C** disappoint	**D** unable
5	**A** methods	**B** routines	**C** processes	**D** ways
6	**A** Look	**B** Focus	**C** Highlight	**D** Point
7	**A** waste	**B** pollution	**C** outcome	**D** emissions
8	**A** almost	**B** much	**C** completely	**D** nearly
9	**A** up	**B** across	**C** over	**D** in
10	**A** innovative	**B** imaginary	**C** inventive	**D** current

9.1 Innovation

VOCABULARY

Describing products

1 Do you agree with this quotation?

'When the product is right, you don't have to be a great marketer.'
Lee Iacocca, former CEO of Chrysler

2 Look at the pictures below. Describe them, using the words in the box.

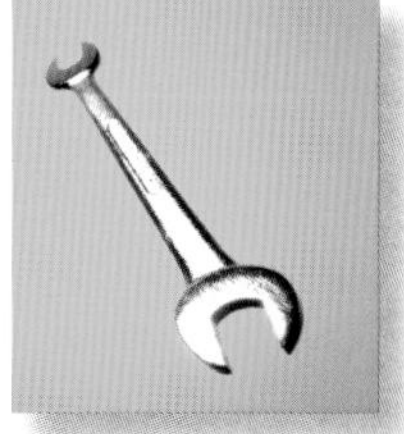

bulky fast state-of-the-art poor old-fashioned basic ~~unwieldy~~ ~~efficient~~ dependable inexpensive small time-consuming ~~practical~~ innovative up-market clever ~~unoriginal~~ ~~erratic~~ over-priced impractical

Now complete the table using the words in the box.

Positive quality	Similar quality	Negative quality
1 a functional tool	practical	________
2 a neat solution	________	unwieldy
3 a modern design	________	________
4 a value-for-money product	________	________
5 a reliable machine	________	erratic
6 a professional service	efficient	________
7 a revolutionary idea	________	unoriginal
8 a quick process	________	________
9 a luxury product	________	________
10 a compact piece of equipment	________	________

3 Choose six items from the table and think of examples from your own experience for each one.

Deleting 'spam' from your email inbox is a time-consuming process.

SPEAKING

Market research

4 9.1 Listen to this example of a telemarketing call. What is the marketer trying to find out?

5 Work with a partner and act out similar conversations. Use the list below and add <u>two</u> more brands of your own.

Brand	First-hand experience?	Positive impression	Negative impression
Dell Computers			
Google			
Mercedes Benz			
The Post Office			

GRAMMAR

Collocations: verb + preposition

6 **Look at these expressions used to describe a new product. Put the correct preposition in each gap.**

0 It is designed *to* withstand high temperatures.
1 It retails ________ $20.
2 It consists ________ two main parts.
3 It comes ________ two different sizes.
4 It is aimed ________ the youth market.
5 It will appeal ________ students.
6 It complies ________ industry standards.
7 It is sold mainly ________ hardware stores.
8 It runs ________ mains electricity.

7 **Think of a product and use four or five of the expressions in exercise 6 to describe it. See if your partner can guess what the product is from these statements.**

They retail at about $40. They come in a range of sizes and colours. They are aimed at the youth market mainly, although some older people wear them too. They are sold in sports shops. They are designed to be light and comfortable.

(Answer: training shoes)

LISTENING

A product presentation

8 9.2 **You work for Greenscope, a company that makes gardening products. You will hear one of your colleagues, a product manager, presenting a product he thinks will revolutionise your business. The first time you listen, complete the notes.**

1 Name of product: ____________________
2 Function: ____________________
3 Target market: ____________________
4 Retail price: ____________________

9 9.2 **Listen again and answer the questions below.**

1 What kind of products would he prefer to sell?
   A Luxury products.
   B Basic products.
   C Products which fulfil a real need.
2 How did the inventor get the idea?
   A He kept over-watering his plants.
   B He had no-one to care for his plants when he was away.
   C His apartment wasn't a good place for growing plants.
3 How have the R&D department improved the original idea?
   A It has a bigger capacity.
   B It can be programmed to water plants more precisely.
   C It comes with detailed plant care instructions.
4 Which market will Plant-carer be targeted at?
   A The general public.
   B Amateur gardeners.
   C Professional gardeners.
5 What does he think is the significance of this product to the company?
   A It will be as successful as the iPod was.
   B It will help them through a period of change.
   C It will give the company a big boost.

READING

1 Which of these statements about innovation do you agree with?

1 'Innovation comes from the producer – not from the customer.'
W. Edwards Deming, business advisor and author

2 'Unless we're in touch with our customers, our model of the world can diverge from reality. There's no substitute for innovation, of course, but innovation is no substitute for being in touch, either.'
Steve Ballmer, CEO Microsoft

2 Take five minutes to read the article on innovation, on page 89, taken from a business newspaper. Is the author saying companies should spend less on research and development (R&D)?

Exam Success

Readthestatements quickly first before reading the article. It will increase your curiosity about the content of the article.

3 Study the article again and answer these questions.

- Which paragraph (**A**, **B**, **C**, **D** or **E**) does each statement (**1–8**) refer to?
- Next to each statement mark one letter (**A**, **B**, **C**, **D** or **E**).
- You will need to use some of these letters more than once.

1 You have to be sure your innovation will last and can go on differentiating your offer.
2 You can innovate with services and business processes as well as with products.
3 Managers are wrong to see innovation as the answer to business growth.
4 Innovations are only successful if consumers like them.
5 Companies who start to innovate must be brave enough to go all the way.
6 You can't measure the success of a company's innovations by its R&D expenditure.
7 Companies innovate because they want to do something different from their competitors.
8 There is no fixed amount you should spend on innovation in order to be competitive.

4 Find these phrasal verbs in the text. Then match each with a definition (A–E).

1 to come up with	A to finish the job
2 to keep up with	B to think of
3 to see something through	C to adopt / to begin to use
4 to take something up	D to stay at the same level as
5 to stand up to	E to be able to resist

SPEAKING

5 Work with a partner and answer these questions.

1 Have you ever come up with an idea for a new product or service?
2 Do you keep up with developments in computing and telecommunications technology?
3 Is there a project you have undertaken that you a) have and b) haven't seen through to the end?
4 Do you sometimes find it difficult to stand up to people when they put pressure on you?
5 Have you taken up any new hobbies or interests in the last three years?

Don't waste your money on *innovation*

A General Motors has invested more money in research and development (R&D) projects in the last 25 years than any other big corporation. But at the same time, its market share has declined. The fact is that there is no correlation between the amount of revenue spent on R&D and the innovative success of an organisation. Managers who think that innovation is a passport to greater market share and profitability are fooling themselves. A recent survey by the respected consulting firm, Booz Allen, found that among the world's top 1,000 corporate R&D spenders there was 'no discernible statistical relationship between R&D spending levels and nearly all measures of business success including sales growth, gross profit, operating profit, enterprise profit, market capitalisation or total shareholder return.'

B But this should not come as any surprise. The level of R&D spending – whether in euros, dollars or a percentage of sales – is not a measure of effectiveness or productivity. The ability to come up with new ideas, to be creative or to innovate is not a question of budgetary investment. The real driver of innovation is growing market competition, not growing R&D spending. The definition of a successful innovation policy is when companies are able to make a cost-effective investment to differentiate themselves from their competitors. If that comes about by a 1% investment of revenue in R&D, then good luck to the company. If it takes 10% to keep up with or stay ahead of the competition, that is fine, too.

C This doesn't necessarily mean product innovation. The Dell Computers model is a good example. Dell spend very little on product innovation – they leave that to others in the industry. In this respect they seem to be more a follower than a leader. Their principal innovation, and now their core competence, is in supply chain management. By producing locally and by selling direct to the consumer online and by telephone, they have been able to manage their costs in a way that means the model works anywhere in the world, from the UK to China.

D But creating an innovative product or model is not sufficient. It's sustaining that difference that is really the key to successful innovation. Few companies, in fact, are able to make that step. Once they have innovated to find a competitive advantage, all too often they lack the courage to see them through. To be a successful innovator you don't need to be rich, but you do need to be incredibly bold. Any film producer knows this: a low-budget independent film, well marketed and well timed has every chance of being as successful as a $100m Hollywood blockbuster.

E After all, there are no prizes for the number of patents granted. Countries and companies who measure their success on how much money they 'invest in the future' are missing the point. Your innovation is only a good one if customers respond to it and take it up. The real measure of productivity is how many new customers you gain and how many profitable existing ones you are able to retain. Apple's iPod is, on the face of it, a fantastic innovation, a product of a company that spends less than the industry average on R&D. But in the end its success will be measured by how well it stands up to its many competitors and whether Apple are able to establish their i-tunes store as the place to purchase and download music and other media content.

Idioms

1 9.3 **You will hear an extract from an internal meeting between two managers at a software developer. They are discussing a job they have been offered. Are they going to accept the job?**

2 9.3 **The speakers use a lot of idiomatic phrases. Listen again and complete the phrases below.**

1 The only _________ block is the price.
2 You're assuming that we've got to start from _________ .
3 There's no need to reinvent the _________ .
4 You imagine it's all going to be _________ sailing.
5 The costs have _________ out of control.
6 Of course there would be _________ problems.
7 I'm sure we can find some middle _________ with them.
8 If it all goes pear-_________, don't say I didn't warn you.

3 **Work with a partner. How would you express each idea in your language? Is there a similar idiom or one that is very different?**

GRAMMAR

would

4 **Look at these pairs of sentences. How are the sentences with *would* different?**

1	I want a diet coke.	A	I would like a diet coke, please.
2	That's out of the question.	B	That would be very difficult for us.
3	Ican'tagreebeforespeakingtomy boss.	C	I would need to speak to my manager before agreeing anything.
4	Can you give us a discount?	D	Would you be prepared to offer us a discount?
5	Please do what you can to help.	E	I would appreciate any help you can offer.

5 **Transform these sentences using *would* and the words given in brackets to make them sound more diplomatic.**

0 A written contract means there will be no misunderstanding. (prevent)
A written contract **would prevent any** misunderstanding.
1 We can move a little on price if you increase the order. (prepared)
2 Can you deliver 1,000 units to us as soon as possible? (able)
3 We can't accept the terms you propose. (have difficulty)
4 Consider it from our point of view. (ask you)
5 Manufacturing only 100 doesn't make any sense. (viable)
6 I don't want to give you an answer now. (like to think)
7 What is in the deal for our company? (benefit)

WRITING

A letter in response to a request

6 You are the manager of an office cleaning company. You have received this request from a client. What does he want?

15 October

Dear Sir / Madam

As Property Manager at Spatcol, I am responsible for the maintenance, cleaning and servicing of all our offices in the UK. We have recently moved our headquarters out of central London to a business park near Uxbridge.

We are looking for a firm to manage the following services for our new facility:

- cleaning and plant care;
- security and car parking attendants;
- basic maintenance of electrical installations (lighting, lifts, etc);
- upkeep of the surrounding gardens and green areas.

I am attaching full specifications of our offices. Please submit your proposal to me, David Ferguson, Head of Property Services Division, at the above address by 12 November.

Yours faithfully

David Ferguson

David Ferguson

Learning Tip

When writing, don't make claims you cannot justify. So if, for example, you claim to offer the highest quality services, then give examples and references to support this.

7 You ask your assistant manager to write a reply. When you check it, you find that it is too direct and not polite enough. Change it so that it sounds more diplomatic and encouraging to the customer.

TOP OFFICE CLEANING

Dear Mr Ferguson

Thanks for your letter asking us to quote for the contract for office cleaning, maintenance and security at Spatcol.

I don't know how you got our name, but we are really only an office cleaning company. We do a bit of garden maintenance, but the other jobs you mention are not our field. If you like we could just take on the office cleaning and garden maintenance work and leave the other jobs to another company. I don't see any problem with that. If that's not what you had in mind, then I suppose you'd be better off with a company that can do it all.

Sorry not to be of more help this time, but do think of us again for cleaning work if you have another building and are looking for cleaners. We do a good job and have a lot of satisfied customers.

Best wishes

Paul Gunson

Paul Gunson

9.2 Negotiating

READING

1 Read the following extract from *Getting past no* by Willam Ury. How could the AT&T negotiator have avoided this breakdown in communication?

An AT&T sales team was negotiating to sell Boeing a new telecommunications system valued at $150 million. The sales team made a persuasive pitch on the kind of service to be delivered, the company's prompt response to problems, and the speed of repairs.

Then the Boeing purchasing director said, 'Fine. Now put each one of your promises in writing. And we want guarantees that if the system isn't fixed on time, you'll pay us damages.'

'We'll make our best efforts,' replied the AT&T sales chief, 'but we can't be held liable for all the things that can go wrong. Lightning can strike ...'

'You're fooling around with us!' interrupted the Boeing negotiator, losing his temper. 'First you tell us about your services – now you're not willing to commit yourself to what you promised!'

'That's not true!' protested the sales chief, aghast at the turn in the negotiation. 'Let me see if I can explain ...' But the Boeing negotiator refused to listen. 'You're not negotiating in good faith!' he complained. 'We can't deal with you.'

2 Read the advice that William Ury gives following this story. Do you agree with it? Are there situations where you simply cannot continue negotiating?

To break through your opponent's resistance you need to reverse the dynamic. If you want him to listen to you, begin by listening to him. If you want him to acknowledge your point, acknowledge his first. To get him to agree with you, begin by agreeing with him wherever you can.

3 Study the following phrases. Which do you think would have been a good response to the Boeing executive's request to put all his promises in writing?

A 'That would be no problem for us.'
B 'I think we both know that in practice that would be almost impossible to work out.'
C 'I think that's a fair request and I'll see what we can do.'
D 'In principle, that sounds OK, but I would have to speak to my people before agreeing the details.'
E 'OK, but what would you be able to do for us in return?'
F 'Interesting question, but just put yourself in our shoes and I think you know the answer.'

4 Write your own response.

SPEAKING

Business angels: a negotiation

5 This is a negotiation between entrepreneurs who have a new product to develop and business angels who are looking for investment opportunities.

- Work in groups of four (two entrepreneurs and two business angels).
- Read the instructions for your group below and decide which aspects of the product each of you is going to present (entrepreneurs) or to ask about (angels).
- Prepare for the meeting.

Entrepreneurs

The product
You have developed a lightweight paper parasol. It has a telescopic cardboard handle so that it can be carried or planted in the ground to give protection from the sun. It is cheap to manufacture ($1 per unit) and could retail at just $6. The design has an international patent.

The market
It can be used at all types of outdoor summer events: picnics, garden parties, music festivals, sporting events, etc. It can be printed in one of four standard designs or with a custom-made design. So an event sponsor could have his own corporate logo and message printed on it. You expect to sell 50,000 units in the first year.

Your needs
You are looking for an investment of $120,000 to build a management team and to market the product. You are prepared to sell 20% of the company for this investment. You would also welcome the advice of the business angels in how best to bring the product to market.

Business angels
You each invest on average $2 million per year in new product innovations and start-ups. Of these only 15% are successful. You always try to protect your investment by: either selling the business quickly if the products do not take off, or by investing with another business angel.
With any new proposal you need to know the following:

- the value of the product at the moment (patents, any sales or contracts to date).
- the potential size of the market for the product.
- the ability of the entrepreneurs to sell their idea.
- the ability of the entrepreneurs to manage the company.

6 Did you reach an agreement? Which factors were most important when reaching your decision? What did you think of the negotiating style of the other side?

9.3 Reading and Listening Tests: Part Three

EXAM FORMAT

Part Three of the Reading Test and Listening Test practise the same skill: your ability to interpret the main ideas being communicated and to find an answer which paraphrases what is actually written or said.

Part Three of the Reading Test is a long business-related article or text (500–600 words) followed by six 4-option multiple choice questions. Part Three of the Listening Test is a dialogue with two or more speakers followed by eight 3-option multiple choice questions.

This section uses the Reading Test as an example.

APPROACH

Follow these steps.

- Read the instructions twice and make sure you understand the context of the passage and what you are being asked to do.
- Skim read the text for two minutes to get the general idea, paying most attention to the first and last paragraphs.
- Read the first question and identify key words that will lead you to the answer in the text.
- Formulate your own answer to the question before looking at the four choices.
- Choose the answer closest to your own.
- Repeat this procedure for each question.

KEY SKILL

Key words

Exam Success

Reading
Train yourself to answer each question before looking at the four choices. This will help you to be less distracted by the wrong answers.

Listening
As with all parts of the listening test, use the time before the conversation is played to study the questions.

1 Look at the question below and decide what the key words in it are.

1 Why does the author say that it's useful to talk to people in the industry?

2 Now go to the part of the passage where these key word(s) appear and look for the information that provides the answer. Write down your own answer.

> Your idea is probably not new. Just because you haven't seen it in the market doesn't mean much. It could be available in another country, through another sales channel that you are not familiar with, like a specialised mail order company. It's quite possible that your idea has already been tried and failed (for market or technology reasons that still hold true). The only way to find that out is to talk to industry experts.

3 Look at the four choices. Which is closest to your answer?

A to get advice on how to market and sell your product
B to find out in which countries the product could be successful
C to find out if the product has been developed before
D to take advantage of their technical knowledge

EXAM PRACTICE

4 Following the approach described above, do Reading Test Part Three on page 95.

PART THREE

- Read the following article about 'deal design' in negotiating and the questions that follow it.
- For each question **1–6**, choose the best answer **(A, B, C** or **D)**

Traditionally, when we negotiate we're advised to find win–win agreements by searching for common ground. While identifying common ground almost always helps, many of the most frequently overlooked sources of value in agreement arise from differences among the parties. 'Deal design' principles can systematically point to agreements that create value by dovetailing differences.

For example, when two countries were negotiating over a disputed piece of land, they could not agree where to draw the boundaries. When negotiators went beyond the opposing positions, however, they uncovered a vital difference of underlying interest and priority: Country A cared more about security, while Country B cared more about sovereignty. The solution was a demilitarised zone under Country B's flag.

Differences of interest or priority can open the door to unbundling different elements and giving each party what it values the most at the least cost to the other (as the two countries did): a core principle of deal design. A good win–win negotiator may well come up with such creative agreements through focusing on interests, not positions, and brainstorming options. The distinctive contribution of deal design, however, is to crystallise and much more systematically develop the underlying principles.

Let's look at an example of another kind of difference. Suppose an entrepreneur who is genuinely optimistic about the prospects of her fast-growing electronics components company faces a potential buyer who likes the company but is much more sceptical about the company's future cash flow. They negotiate in good faith, but at the end of the day, the two sides sharply disagree on the likely future of the company and so cannot find an acceptable sale price.

Instead of seeing these different forecasts as a barrier, a savvy deal designer would perceive opportunities to bridge the 'value gap'. One option would be a deal in which the buyer pays a fixed amount now and a contingent amount later, with the latter amount determined by the future performance of the company.

Properly structured, such a contingent payment (or 'earn-out') can appear quite valuable to the optimistic seller – who expects to get that earn-out – but not very costly to the less optimistic buyer. The seller's willingness to accept such a contingent deal, moreover, may give the buyer the confidence he or she needs to go through with the deal.

A host of other differences make up the raw material that skilled deal designers transform into joint gains. For example, a less risk-averse party can 'insure' a more risk-averse one. A more impatient party can get more of the early money, while his more patient counterpart can get considerably more over a longer period. Differences in cost or revenue structure, tax status, or regulatory arrangements between two parties can be converted into gains for both. If one party mainly cares about how a deal looks, while the other focuses on substance, the right deal design can create value for both. Indeed, for a savvy deal designer, conducting a disciplined 'differences inventory' is at least as important a task as identifying areas of common ground.

1 The benefit of using 'deal design' principles in negotiating are that
- **A** they focus on shared interests.
- **B** they help people to forget their differences.
- **C** they focus on differences and how to reconcile them.
- **D** they bring a completely fresh approach to negotiating.

2 The focus of the negotiation over the piece of disputed land was
- **A** how to make the area secure.
- **B** where the border between the two countries should be.
- **C** who would control this area.
- **D** which flag would fly over the area.

3 The solution of a demilitarised zone under Country B's flag worked because
- **A** it accommodated the different needs and goals of each party.
- **B** both sides were forced to compromise.
- **C** a new boundary was drawn.
- **D** it was based on fundamental principles.

4 In the example of the electronics company, the owner and the potential buyer have different opinions about
- **A** what kind of business the company should be involved in.
- **B** who will run the business.
- **C** how well the company will perform in the next few years.
- **D** whether they need to trust each other.

5 One suggested way to bridge the differences between them would be to
- **A** link the amount paid for the company to its future financial results.
- **B** persuade the buyer to be more optimistic about its future performance.
- **C** fix on an amount between the asking price and the offer price.
- **D** pay the amount in instalments.

6 It's the job of deal designers to make joint gains out of the two parties'
- **A** raw materials.
- **B** risks.
- **C** income structure.
- **D** differences.

10.1 Travel and entertainment

VOCABULARY

Business travel

1 Do you agree with this view?

'I can see a trend, executives want to save costs on business travel, and connecting people virtually is becoming more affordable.'

Wendy Wong, Polycom

2 Study the phrases in the box. What does each one mean? How is it pronounced?

commute subsidised transport congestion give a lift to someone
rush hour teleconferencing car share scheme travel expenses

3 Which of these statements do you sympathise with?

1 Spending two hours each day commuting to and from work really affects people's quality of life.
2 It's fair that the company should subsidise travel for people who commute a long way to work.
3 If more people worked flexibly we could avoid congestion and rush hours.
4 I don't mind giving a colleague a lift to work now and then but I couldn't take part in a car share scheme. I enjoy that hour to myself in the mornings.
5 Air travel is too time-consuming. Video and teleconferencing is the only way forward.
6 It's the duty of every employee to manage their business travel expenses as if it were their own money.

Learning Tip

Try to use idiomatic phrases when expressing opinions: eg *I couldn't agree more; I'd go along with that; Actually, that's not the way I see it*, etc

4 Discuss the following questions.

1 How do you get to work / college each day?
2 Why do you use this form of transport?
3 Do you pay for your own travel?

5 As the new manager of the support services at Sterrman, an engineering firm, you have been asked to reduce spending on travel and entertainment. Suggest a policy to tackle each of the problems below.

Current situation

1 The company owns and maintains a fleet of 35 company cars for the sales team.
2 The company pays for business class tickets on both long and short flights.
3 The use of expensive restaurants to entertain guests and clients is very common.
4 The company spends a lot on hiring outside rooms for meetings and conferences.

Compare your answers with a partner.

LISTENING

A team-building day

6 **A lot of companies use team-building events, such as canoeing events, treasure hunts, company role plays, etc. But what should their aim be? Prioritise (1–7) the following aims.**

A generally getting to know each other better
B breaking down formal barriers between management and employees
C bringing out the best qualities in each individual
D helping people to feel better about themselves
E distinguishing leaders from followers
F increasing loyalty to the company
G helping to remember that there's more to life than just work

7 **Is there some other benefit that hasn't been mentioned above?**

8 10.1 **Your company has organised a team-building day at Silverstone Motor Racing Circuit. You have been asked to attend a short presentation of the programme for the day. Listen and complete your notes. Use up to three words for each space.**

Team-building day

The aims

0 The aim is not only to have a good time.
1 To learn how each individual thinks, functions and ______________ .
2 This new understanding will make us ______________ .

The schedule

3 Meet at the office at ______________ .
4 The journey will take ______________ .
5 For the activities we will be divided into ______________ .
6 At lunch there will be a surprise ______________ .
7 After the afternoon's activities there will be a ______________ .

Preparation

8 Dress ______________ .
9 In case of cold bring a jumper or ______________ .
10 No mobile phones, laptops, but can bring ______________ .

The home of British Motor Racing

9 **What do you think the activities at the circuit will be exactly?**

GRAMMAR

Future forms

1 Look at the verb forms in these sentences (1–6). What form is used to express the following about the future?

Future forms	
a	an offer
b	a decision already taken
c	an arrangement
d	a schedule
e	a general prediction
f	a confident prediction

1 The day **will begin** with a working breakfast at eight o'clock after which delegates will have 30 minutes of free time before the first seminar at 10 o'clock.
2 **We're not going to have** a Christmas party this year; instead we **are going to give** the money we would have spent to a charity.
3 She's not easy to convince, is she? I can see this **is going to be** a very long discussion.
4 Don't worry, I**'ll take** the laptop with me. That's one less thing for you to remember.
5 **I'm meeting** him at his office at 6.30 and then we**'re eating at** a Greek restaurant in the city centre.
6 I think he**'ll find** it difficult to adapt to his new role, because he's used to being independent.

Learning Tip

Note the use of the present when two clauses about the future are connected with *when* or another time phrase.

I will see him. I will give him your message. ***When I see*** *him, I'll give him your message.*

2 Your colleague has written this email for an agent in Djakarta. Before you send it, she has asked you to put verbs she's not sure about in the most natural form.

Dear Jim

Thank you for your email, asking about our plans for next year.
I **(0)** *will do* my best to explain the situation.

I agree that this year has been disappointing, but we expect that sales **(1)** ________ (pick up) next year. The result of our marketing meeting last week is that we **(2)** ________ (launch) the new version of the DCT10 in Asia next spring. From the feedback we've had in Europe, I'm sure it **(3)** ________ (be) a great success.

The International Gas Industry Trade Fair **(4)** ________ (take place) in Singapore next March. I **(5)** ________ (fly) out there with Jane on 16 March and I hope to have a couple of days extra to see some agents, but I **(6)** ________ (call) you when I **(7)** ________ (have) my exact schedule, so that we can arrange to meet.

In the meantime, let me know if you **(8)** ________ (visit) the UK any time soon. Then we can arrange to meet for a meal and a chat.

Best wishes
Sarah

READING

Events management

3 **Do you think being responsible for organising corporate events, sponsorship, parties and team-building events is a dream job? Why? / Why not?**

4 **Read the article from a business magazine about organising corporate events.**

- Choose the best sentence from those below (**A–H**) to fill each of the gaps in the text.
- Do not use any letter more than once.
- There is an example at the beginning (**0**).

HOW TO MANAGE AN EVENT

Who would be an events organiser? On the face of it, playing 'my genial host' to a group of freeloading clients doesn't seem too arduous a task. But the amount of stress experienced in getting ready for it and the real and ever-present danger of something going horribly wrong make it a job only for those with nerves of steel. (**0**) E The list is endless.

Corporate hospitality events should be an opportunity to relax with your customers and get away from business, but instead they actually expose a company to close scrutiny by its most valued audience and leave a lasting impression in their minds. Done well, the client is left with the image of a creative, fun and professional organisation. (**1**) _____ Worse still, you might offend: the company who arranged a James Bond theme night that started with a group of international guests being greeted by bikini-clad 'Bond girls' should have known better.

The first consideration is what the aim of the event is: to launch a new product, to develop awareness of the company's mission, to build relationships with new clients or just to thank existing ones for their continued custom. (**2**) _____ For the latter you won't necessarily have to spend excessively to get it right, but you will have to think about what will make the event memorable. Audience participation is generally a good way to achieve this, for example giving a theme to the event, such as a 1970s disco or a Hawaiian evening. (**3**) _____ It may also put some under pressure, making them feel that they will have to dance like John Travolta or to rely more on their wallet than their imagination to make their costume. (**4**) _____

An alternative is simply to give them a treat by taking them to a show or sporting event and afterwards for a meal where they can relax and chat. (**5**) _____ The advantage of these is that the clients are more likely to look forward to it and to share the good news with others in the wider world who may also have an interest in the event. (**6**) _____ In addition, anything that goes wrong at the event is likely to reflect badly on the main organiser and not your company.

A This will get the participants more involved and help to 'break the ice' if people don't know each other well, but be careful.

B An example of this would be a golf tournament or a football match.

C The first two are more like presentations and will mean putting on a show to impress.

D Staff parties, on the other hand, are much less stressful because the consequences of failure are not so damaging.

E A speaker may not turn up, a piece of vital equipment may fail, the invitation may give the wrong date.

F Done badly, the company may end up looking cheesy, disorganised or even cheap.

G The result is good publicity and an enhanced image for the company.

H The balance is a difficult one and it all depends on the skill of the organiser in the planning and publicizing of the event, so the guests feel at ease.

VOCABULARY

go and get

1 Complete the following sentences using the correct form of either *go* or *get*.

0 There is always a danger that something will *go* wrong on the day.
1 I have a lot of things to ________ ready before the party tomorrow.
2 The key to a successful event is to ________ all the participants involved.
3 I can't do 13 July, I'm afraid – it's the day my brother is ________ married.
4 Don't worry. Everything is ________ according to plan.
5 Can you call them, please? I've tried to convince them, but I'm not ________ anywhere.
6 The budget for this event is out of control. The company will ________ bankrupt at this rate.
7 The boss will ________ crazy if he finds out you've taken his parking space.
8 Everything went smoothly, except for the three people who ________ lost on their way from the airport.

2 Choose four of the above phrases with *go* or *get* and write sentences of your own.

READING

Planning a corporate event

3 You work for Vermillion Events Management, which specialises in organising conferences and corporate events. You receive the following letter. Read it and with your partner agree an outline plan for the event using the framework given on page 101.

CATHSTONE
DESIGNERS OF FINE JEWELLERY

Dear Sir / Madam

Cathstone will be celebrating its 50th anniversary in business this November and would like to organise a suitable event to commemorate the occasion. Your company was recommended to me by a colleague.

In case you have not heard of us, Cathstone is Asia's leading jewellery designer and wholesaler. We supply prestige jewellers in major cities across the world.

Attending the event will be the senior management team (30 people) and about 200 of our key clients and suppliers with their husbands, wives or partners.

I don't need to stress to you the importance of putting on a good show, but we leave it to you to come up with a proposal for what the theme and venue might be. We have set aside a reasonable budget for the event, but of course we are not handing you a blank cheque! Please submit a rough estimate of cost with your proposal. I look forward to hearing from you.

Yours faithfully

Martha Lorax
Martha Lorax
Communications Director

Outline proposal for corporate event	
1 Company	__________
2 Purpose of event	__________
3 Venue	__________
4 Theme	__________
5 Speakers / Guests	__________
6 Activities	__________
7 Food and drink	__________
8 Promotional literature / gifts	__________
9 Approx. cost per head	__________

SPEAKING

Exam Success

Practisemakingbrief notes that you can refer to when giving a short speech or contributing at a meeting.

Making a pitch

4 **You have been invited to pitch for the customer event at Cathstone. Divide yourself into pairs of events managers and a panel of Cathstone managers. Read the instructions below and then act out the meeting.**

Events Managers

Present your ideas for the event to the Cathstone panel. Divide the presentation into two parts so that each person has equal opportunity to speak. Be prepared to answer questions afterwards.

Panel

First discuss together what you are looking for. Then listen to two or three pitches by different event management companies. After each pitch, ask questions. At the end decide who is the winner and be prepared to give our reasons.

10.2 The language of proposals

LISTENING

Taking notes

1 10.2 **At the end of their six-month trial period working in a consultancy company, two trainees are called to a meeting with their manager. Listen to what he asks them to do and take careful notes on his instructions.**

1 Project: ______________________
2 Aims: ______________________
3 Deadline: ______________________
4 Resources: ______________________

2 **Compare your notes with a partner.**

READING

3 **Look at the two proposals below. Which one best answers the manager's request?**

To: Geoffrey Bindstock
From: Claudia Hermann
Re: Improvements to the work environment

Further to discussions with various employees and an analysis of the use of space in the offices and its compatibility with the work carried out here, I would like to make the following observations and recommendations.

Observations

1 The offices are well laid out and although not everyone has his / her own desk, the use of space is very efficient.
2 The open plan office can be noisy and this is distracting when you are making a telephone call.
3 The decoration is quite functional and a bit impersonal, but people are able to do their work perfectly well.

Recommendations

In order to improve this work environment and address these issues, I would like to make the following recommendations:

1 The open plan layout should remain, but the firm should invest in headphones for each telephone so that calls can be taken without distraction.

2 Some consideration should be given to making the space less impersonal and staff should be consulted on how to do this.

The advantages of these measures are that they are inexpensive and involve little disruption to normal busines. Please consider these options and do not hesitate to contact me for further details.

Proposal for improvement of the work area

I asked myself three questions when considering how well the present office space works: Is it efficiently used? Is it comfortable and convenient? And is it a motivating place to work in?

The first question seems to have been addressed by the management. The sharing of desks means that little space is wasted and the limited availability of meeting rooms means that consultants arrange outside meetings wherever possible, so saving the firm valuable money.

The answers to the second and third questions are less satisfactory. The desks and space are functional and well equipped, although there are too few meeting rooms. This is especially a problem when people need to have a confidential call or meeting.

The other result of no-one having his / her own space is that there is no possibility to personalise it by putting up photos or pictures. This is demotivating and reduces staff loyalty to the space and therefore the firm.

To solve these issues, I suggest that the office space be converted into semi-open plan. That is to say, partitions are introduced around groups of 3–4 desks so that people can feel more independent and able to decorate their space. To make them more involved, staff should be consulted on colour schemes, who they would like to share with, etc. At the same time four or five new meeting rooms can be created.

I hope this is useful.

David Black

4 **What are the good and bad points about each proposal? Discuss with a partner. Consider the following:**

- style
- tone
- layout

WRITING

A proposal for a corporate event

5 **Study the rules of proposal writing below. Are there any other rules you can add?**

Writing a proposal

1 Say who the proposal is for, what its subject is and who it is from.
To: The Board of Setco
From: Walter Smith
Re: Customer complaints

2 Begin with the reason for writing and a summary of the situation / needs.
The Managing Director has recently highlighted inefficiencies in the way that customer complaints are handled. This proposal aims to identify the problem areas and suggest solutions to them.

3 Divide the proposal into clearly identifiable sections by either numbering each point or by giving it a sub-heading.
- Problems identified
- Reasons for these inefficiencies
- Proposed solutions
- Advantages and disadvantages of each measure

4 Finish with a conclusion that is firm but not too directive.
In summary, our advice is that more specific training in complaints handling be given to a few key personnel. Limiting the number of staff who receive the training will keep the cost down.

Learning Tip

The more you read, the better you will write. Find examples of each type of business communication (eg letters, reports, proposals) to read and learn from.

6 **Write a proposal for the Cathstone corporate event, based on what you decided on page 101. Use the framework below.**

Proposal for corporate event
To: Martha Lorax
From:
Re:
- Introduction
- Proposed event
- Reasons for choice of venue and theme
- Promotional aspects
- Catering
- Cost
- Conclusion

10.3

Speaking Test: Part Three

EXAM FORMAT

Part Three of the Speaking Test is a discussion between two or three candidates, followed by questions put to the candidates by the interlocutor on the same topic. The topic for discussion will be given to you on a card (eg discuss ways to introduce a suggestion scheme at work). The idea is to simulate a business meeting between colleagues.

This part tests your ability to interact with others in a business situation, using appropriate functional language (agreeing, making suggestions, justifying, etc). It will last about five minutes.

APPROACH

Follow these steps.

- You have 30 seconds to read the instructions and topic for discussion. Read it very carefully.
- Begin the discussion by introducing the topic and subjects for discussion. This will allow you time to make sure you understand the topic.
- Give your partner the opportunity to speak and comment on what they say – by agreeing or disagreeing, adding points, etc.
- When the interlocutor stops you and asks questions, make sure you understand each question before answering. Ask for clarification if necessary.

KEY SKILL

Structuring a discussion

Exam Success

Don't think about what you *think* the examiner wants you to say; say what you want to say about the topic. The more natural your contribution is, the better you will express it. In other words, treat the task as realistically as possible.

1 To stimulate a business discussion it will help to know some relevant phrases. What would you say to ...?

0 begin the discussion	*Shall we begin?*
1 give the background	As ________
2 give your own opinion	As I ________
3 invite your partner's opinion	What ________
4 make a suggestion	One idea ________
5 praise your partner's suggestion	That's ________
6 disagree politely	I see ________
7 interrupt	Could ________
8 summarise what is agreed	So, just to ________

Check your answers by looking at the language box on page 105.

EXAM PRACTICE

2 **Work in pairs. Study the situation task sheet below for 30 seconds and discuss the situation together. Look at the phrases below which will help you to structure your discussion.**

Task sheet 1

Transport Initiative

(For two candidates)

In order to limit its impact on the environment, your company would like to discourage so many employees from driving their cars to work. Instead it wants to promote the use of car sharing and of public transport. You have been asked to make some recommendations for this scheme.

Discuss, and decide together:

- how you would promote such a scheme within the company
- what the costs and benefits would be for the company

Structuring a discussion

OK. Shall we begin? / Let's get started.
As you know, the company would like to ...
So we're here to discuss ...
There are two issues we need to look at:

- Firstly, how to ...
- And secondly ...

Let's look at the first issue. How do you think we can ...?
Well, for me the best way is ...
As I see it, we should ...
What do you think?
That's an excellent idea.
I see your point, but ...
I agree but there's one point I'd like to add.
I think that's one possibility. Another would be to ...
So, just to sum up, we've agreed that we should ...

3 **Use the examiner's questions to continue the discussion.**

1. Do you think companies evaluate properly the cost of business travel in time and money?
2. Should public transport always be subsidised by government? Why? / Why not?
3. Why is it so difficult to persuade people to stop using their cars to get to work?
4. Is it right for companies to get involved in people's individual choices in this way? Why? / Why not?

11.1 The economy

VOCABULARY

Economic issues

1 What does this quotation mean? Do you agree?

'The gap in our economy is between what we have and what we think we ought to have – and that is a moral problem, not an economic one.'
Paul Heyne, Economics lecturer

2 Choose the right word to complete these sentences about the economy.

1 The cost of *life / living* in London is so high now that many people on low *incomes / revenues* find it difficult to live there.
2 Insecurity in the *job / work* market has affected consumer *confidence / trust.*
3 The government has cut a lot of public *segment / sector* jobs and contracted the work out to *private / self-employed* companies.
4 Foreign *investing / investment* in our manufacturing industry has helped economic *growth / growing up.*
5 The unemployment *ratio / rate* in some parts of the country is over 20% and the *benefits / subsidies* that the government pays to the jobless are very high.
6 *Abroad / Foreign* imports are increasing and the country now has a big trade *deficit / shortage.*
7 Competition and a *free / open* market has brought prices down and has increased people's purchasing *power / ability.*
8 The tax *burden / pressure* on companies is so heavy now that many of them are *delocating / relocating* to countries where taxes are lower.

3 Put these words that describe the economy in order from the most positive (++) to the most negative (– –).

stable booming buoyant depressed healthy stagnant

4 Which best describes your country's economy at the moment? What are the reasons for its condition?

5 How does the welfare state work in your country?

1 Are the benefits paid by the state to the unemployed, the disabled, pregnant women and retired people generous or not?
2 Do you think these benefits should be paid by the state or by private insurance?

READING

6 Read the article about the relationship between governments and big business. Is it optimistic about this relationship? Why? / Why not?

Finance Weekly, 10 September

The new philanthropists

The 19th century was the age of capitalism, the 20th century socialism. The 21st century, it seems, will be the age of charity. But, as Mrs Thatcher said, 'The Good Samaritan had to earn his money first.'

Warren Buffett, when he made a gift of $31bn to the Gates Foundation, already worth $29bn, joked that his children would have to work for their living – apart from a billion dollar handout to each.

Later, when Buffet and Gates held a press conference to announce what they intended to do with their fortune, it was clear that channelling it through government was not an option. 'Bill and Melinda will do a better job than ... the Federal Treasury,' said Buffet. Instead they would 'seek out talent to distribute their money just as they sought out talent to acquire it'.

For these tycoons, who have prospered in the free market global economy, government and the public sector are monopolistic and inefficient. Governments may have built the welfare state in the 20th century, but to provide them with free cash to support these structures (schools, hospitals, etc) was not on their agenda. Instead their efforts will be focused on alleviating world poverty and disease, and improving access to technology.

Adam Smith's 'invisible hand', the economic theory that the market will run smoothly if it is left to decide what products are sold and at what price, has been the guiding principle behind globalisation. In America it has produced large fortunes for a handful of successful industrialists: men who now, it seems, are turning to philanthropy.

Opponents say that the free market shows no regard for social concerns and encourages poor employment and environmental standards. Wealth, they argue, is now concentrated among a handful of global corporations whose only interest is financial profit and who are only accountable to their shareholders. They would like to see governments put a brake on the activities of big business.

But the power of governments, national and international, is dwindling. The welfare states of the 20th century, and the public sector workers who staff them, are slowly being replaced – if not by private sector workers, then certainly by private sector principles. Government and public service have become synonymous with inefficiency and waste.

At the same time, the agents of international government – the UN, the IMF, the World Bank and the EU – have subsidised too many dictators and undermined too many economies. As their reputation declines, they will be replaced by the charity of the private sector.

Children of the 60s, like Bill Gates, have exploited the free market ruthlessly, but now they are preaching freedom and love and are choosing to give back to society. Their hearts are in the right place. But they share one enemy – modern government in all its forms. As Buffett said, only a fool gives his money to the treasury.

Will such people make a better world? Who knows? But they mean to try.

READING

1 Read the article on page 107 again and choose the best answer (A, B, C or D) to each question.

1 Warren Buffett's children will
   A not get a penny from their father.
   B get a job with their father.
   C get a billion dollars each.
   D have to earn their money as he did.

2 Who will organise the handing out of Buffett's fortune?
   A Bill and Melinda Gates.
   B Bill Gates and Warren Buffett.
   C The Federal Treasury.
   D People specially employed by Gates and Buffett.

3 What will the money not be spent on?
   A Schools and hospitals in the US.
   B Helping the world's poor people.
   C Helping the world's sick.
   D Providing Internet and communications technology to more people.

4 *Opponents* in the sixth paragraph refers to opponents of
   A multinational companies and their shareholders.
   B the economic system that has produced globalisation.
   C philanthropists like Buffett.
   D the smooth running of the market.

5 What is happening to government, national and international, according to the author?
   A It has become too powerful.
   B It has too many agents.
   C It is becoming corrupt.
   D It is losing influence.

6 What does the phrase *their hearts are in the right place* say about people like Gates and Buffett?
   A Money is not so important to them.
   B They have good intentions.
   C Their actions are damaging.
   D They are led by their emotions.

2 Find a word or phrase in the text which is the opposite of the following.

1 live off your inheritance
2 struggled
3 supporters
4 poverty
5 becoming greater
6 strengthened

3 Do you think that rich philanthropists can do a better job than governments in helping the needy in society?

4 Which of these economic points of view do you agree with?

1 'No society ever prospered by punishing the rich. They are the ones who create wealth in our communities and raise everyone's standard of living.'
2 'Governments should not worry about the rich. The rich will always find a way to look after themselves. It is the job of government to look after the poor in society.'

GRAMMAR

Conditionals (types 1 and 2)

5 What is the difference in meaning between these sentences?

1a If they raise the rate of income tax for top earners, these people will probably leave the country.

1b If they raised the rate of income tax for top earners, these people would probably leave the country.

2a If I earn a lot of money in my career, I will probably also give a lot to charity.

2b If I had as much money as Warren Buffett, I would probably also give a lot to charity.

Conditionals (type 1 and 2)

Note the forms of both types of sentence.
If + present, ... *will* + infinitive (without *to*)
If + past, ... *would* + infinitive (without *to*)

- We use the first type of *if* sentence for situations which are real and possible.
- We use the second for situations which are either unreal or improbable.

6 Decide if the forms used in these sentences are correct or not. If not, correct them.

0 If I am ten years younger, I will ask her to marry me. Incorrect (x)
If I ~~am~~ were ten years younger, I ~~will~~ would ask her to marry me.
1 If I see him, I will certainly give him your message.
2 If I knew the answer to that, I'd be a rich man.
3 If you were going to be late, please would you call me and let me know.
4 If you are in my position, what will you do?
5 We will have to look for another supplier if they continue to raise their prices every three months.
6 I wouldn't do your job unless I was paid a fortune!
7 If I have a better knowledge of finance, I will apply for the job.
8 I will come with you if you promise to do the negotiating yourself.

SPEAKING

Socio-economic problems

7 Which of the following are problems in your country? Decide if they are a *serious problem*, a *slight problem* or *not a problem*.

Problem	Serious problem	Slight problem	Not a problem
1 Income gap between rich and poor			
2 An ageing population and / or pensions crisis			
3 Over-dependence on the welfare state			
4 Unemployment			
5 Shortage of key skills or inadequate education system			
6 Heavy tax burden (on individuals and / or companies)			
7 Homelessness or a shortage of affordable housing			
8 Poor health and diet or a failing health service			
9 Personal debt			
10 Lack of investment in transport, public services, etc			

1 **Discuss the list on page 109 with your partner. What are the main problems? What is the government doing about them?**

2 **What more could they do? Use *if* sentences to make suggestions.**

If the government increased the rate of tax for top earners and reduced the rate for the lowest earners, the gap between rich and poor would become smaller.

READING

3 **You are thinking of relocating to another country to set up a small manufacturing company.**

1 Make a list of the most important factors to consider in deciding where.
2 Compare your list with a partner.

4 **Read the text. What reasons for relocating to Nicaragua does the author highlight?**

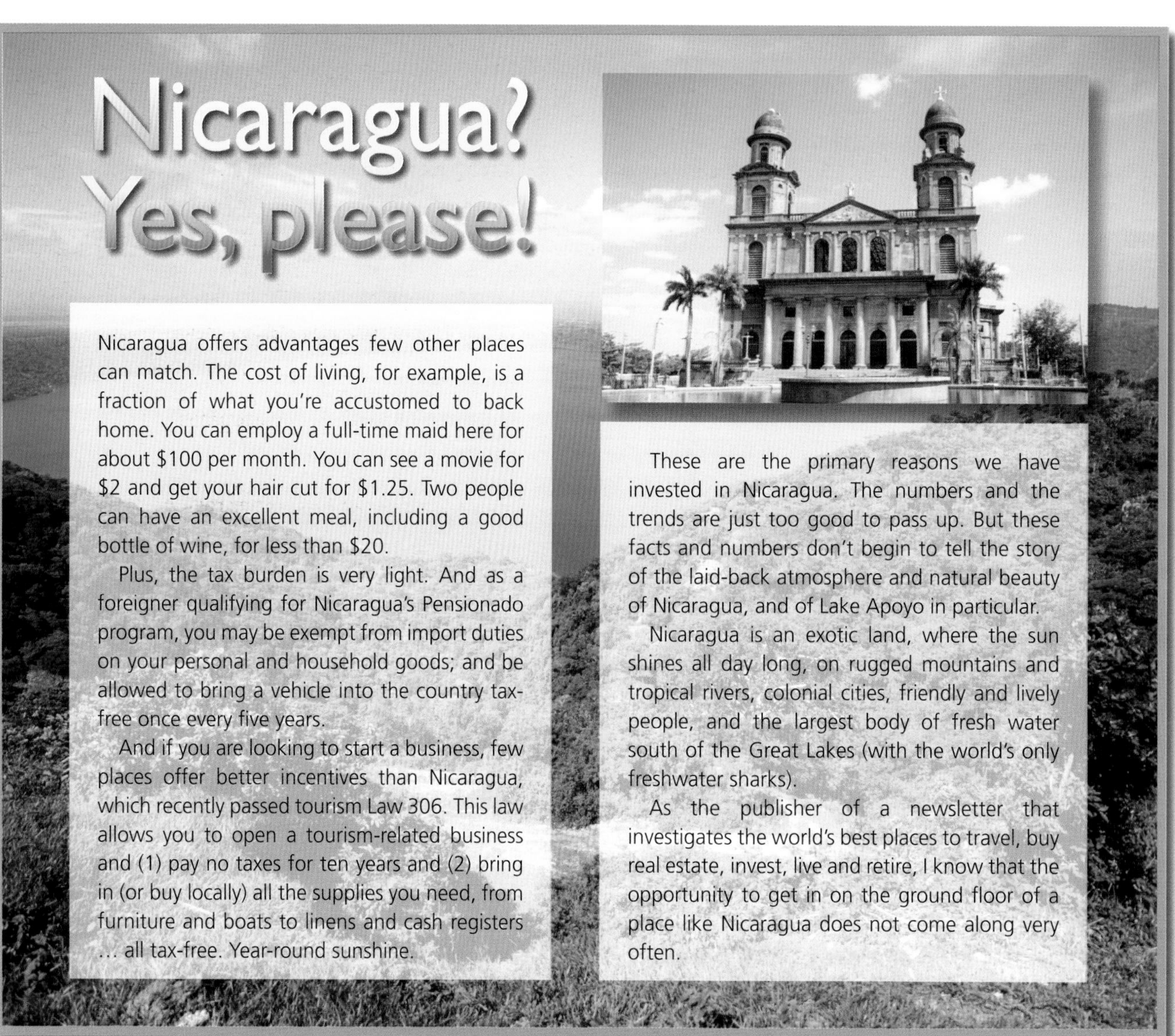

Nicaragua? Yes, please!

Nicaragua offers advantages few other places can match. The cost of living, for example, is a fraction of what you're accustomed to back home. You can employ a full-time maid here for about $100 per month. You can see a movie for $2 and get your hair cut for $1.25. Two people can have an excellent meal, including a good bottle of wine, for less than $20.

Plus, the tax burden is very light. And as a foreigner qualifying for Nicaragua's Pensionado program, you may be exempt from import duties on your personal and household goods; and be allowed to bring a vehicle into the country tax-free once every five years.

And if you are looking to start a business, few places offer better incentives than Nicaragua, which recently passed tourism Law 306. This law allows you to open a tourism-related business and (1) pay no taxes for ten years and (2) bring in (or buy locally) all the supplies you need, from furniture and boats to linens and cash registers … all tax-free. Year-round sunshine.

These are the primary reasons we have invested in Nicaragua. The numbers and the trends are just too good to pass up. But these facts and numbers don't begin to tell the story of the laid-back atmosphere and natural beauty of Nicaragua, and of Lake Apoyo in particular.

Nicaragua is an exotic land, where the sun shines all day long, on rugged mountains and tropical rivers, colonial cities, friendly and lively people, and the largest body of fresh water south of the Great Lakes (with the world's only freshwater sharks).

As the publisher of a newsletter that investigates the world's best places to travel, buy real estate, invest, live and retire, I know that the opportunity to get in on the ground floor of a place like Nicaragua does not come along very often.

5 **What is meant by these phrases in the text?**

1 advantages few other places can match
2 exempt from import duties
3 too good to pass up
4 the laid-back atmosphere
5 get in on the ground floor

LISTENING

Relocation experiences

6 11.1 **Listen to these five people talking about their experiences of relocating home or business.**

- The first time you listen, indicate the **reason** for the move.
- The second time, indicate what **problem** arose that they did not expect.

TASK ONE – REASON

1 ______	A	cheaper labour costs
	B	lower local taxes for companies
2 ______	C	better climate
	D	better quality of life
3 ______	E	expansion
4 ______	F	shorter travel time to work
	G	to be closer to suppliers
5 ______	H	cheaper living costs

TASK TWO – PROBLEM

6 ______	A	having to travel long distances
	B	customers are further away
7 ______	C	not much to do in the evenings
	D	some wasted space
8 ______	E	it's no cheaper than other regions
9 ______	F	it's sometimes noisy
	G	workers are poorly skilled
10 ______	H	cost of living is rising

7 **What do these expressions from the listening passage mean?**

1 it was *just a carrot* to get people to move here
2 it's ten minutes away, which is really *handy*
3 without *giving it a second thought*
4 the salary bill is *creeping up*
5 we decided to *take the plunge*
6 you can't *have it both ways*

8 **What / Where would be your ideal place to live and work? Why?**

11.2 Effective writing

WRITING

Learning Tip

For written business communication to be effective there are three important things to remember:

- be organised
- be to the point
- be appropriate

Written business communication

1 **Read the Learning Tip then look at these three short extracts. Each one succeeds in two of the important ways to be effective but fails in the other. Identify the weakness of each one.**

A

Dear Mr Song

I'm writing this for Professor Olsen, who's away on sabbatical at the moment. He's asked me to thank you for your offer of an honorary doctorate at Seoul University. He says that he is sorry but he'll have to say no this time because his diary is so full of other commitments.

Please don't take this the wrong way. It's not a reflection on what he thinks of your university. It is just that …

B

The purpose of this report is to set out the findings of the finance committee into potential overseas investments and make recommendations accordingly. The investments we recommend most strongly are in the mining industry in the fast-growing economy of Namibia. The reason for this is that the government of Namibia has recognised the opportunities for development and invested large sums in the country's infrastructure. The scope of our research was worldwide, although we tended to look more closely at emerging countries and markets, since our brief was to look for industries with a high and fast return. The only drawbacks of this potential investment are the uncertainties inherent in the industry itself …

C

In response to a request from the managing director to find ways of improving communications within the organisation, we have prepared the following proposal.

Our first meeting with the managing director was in June. During this meeting, we were asked to analyse the current situation, in which communications were not working as effectively as they should, and to present ideas for a better exchange of information between departments and individuals. Since not all members of the project team could be present, a second meeting was held to pass on the information about the project.

Our analysis involved evaluating the current situation: monitoring the work of several closely-linked departments and seeing how they communicated with each other …

2 **Work in groups of three. Each choose one of the passages to rewrite, correcting its weakness.**

3 **Exchange your rewritten passages and compare.**

WRITING

A delicate letter

4 **Answer the questions below, using this table as a guide.**

Effective writing	
How to be organised	Plan your writing, dividing it into clear sections / paragraphs and considering what emphasis to give to each part.
How to be to the point	Think of the most economical way to say what you want and then put it into an appropriate form.
How to be appropriate	Consider your relationship to the reader (formal or informal). Always be polite. Only make claims you can support with examples.

5 **Write a brief plan for the following letter.**

You have been employing a consultant to help you improve your marketing. She has been working with you for two months but up to now has told you nothing that you did not know already. You have decided to terminate the contract with her (she will be paid for the work done so far). Write to her to explain.

6 **Write as simply and directly as possible the reason for terminating her contract. Then put this statement into more diplomatic language.**

7 **Look at the following beginning to the letter and put it into a more appropriate style.**

> Dear Madam,
>
> It is two months since you were first commissioned to provide us with marketing assistance.

Read the following claim and give an example to support it.

> The advice you gave us in your first report was straight from a marketing textbook.

8 **Plan and write the letter for the following situation.**

You work as sales manager for a company which makes labels and signs. Two months ago you agreed a lucrative contract with a garden centre to make labels for the trees they sell. After delivering the first batch of 20,000 labels, you received a complaint that the ink on the labels was not waterproof. The customer now wants to cancel the contract and to be refunded for the labels already paid for.
You would like to rescue the contract and to limit the loss on the 20,000 labels which you have already supplied.

11.3 Speaking Test: Part Two

EXAM FORMAT

Part Two of the Speaking Test consists of a one-minute presentation by each candidate followed by a discussion. It lasts about six minutes in total. The presentations are based on a choice of three topics given to you by the examiner, each requiring a different level of business knowledge or experience – from general to experienced. You have one minute to make notes and prepare your presentation. This part of the exam tests your ability to organise your ideas and present them as if in a business meeting.

APPROACH

Exam Success

Aminuteisonlylong enough to make two or three key points, so don't worry about not having much to say.

Follow these steps.

- Read the three topics carefully and quickly decide the one you would like to talk about.
- Note down two or three key arguments (you will not have time to develop more than this).
- Give your presentation a clear introduction and ending. Paraphrase the question on your prompt card to introduce the subject (see below).
- At the end invite your partner to comment on what you have said.
- Listen carefully to your partner's presentation and be ready to comment on it.

KEY SKILL

Organising your thoughts

1 Look at the topic and the example notes below.

Relocating your company offices: the important factors to consider.

Key points:
- business reasons: how will it improve the business?
- the costs involved
- what impact will it have on employees?

2 Now do the same for the following topics, making brief notes on each one.

1 **International communication**: the importance in business of learning at least a few words of another language.
2 **Effective presentations**: how to involve your audience when giving a presentation.
3 **Leadership**: why good communication skills are an essential quality for a business leader.

3 Compare notes with your partner.

EXAM PRACTICE

4 **Choose one of the topics below and speak about it for a minute. Look at the useful phrases that will help you to organise your presentation.**

> **Customer relations:** the importance of listening carefully to what customers are saying.

> **Communication skills:** giving the right impression at a job interview.

Giving a mini-presentation

So why should we ...
I think there are three important points here.
Firstly, ... Secondly, ... And finally, ...

I'd like to say a few words about ...
Of course, it's important to ...
But on the other hand, ...
There is also the question of ...

I think I've covered the main points ...
Those are my views on it ...
What do you think ...?
Do you agree ...?

Yes. There's just one point I'd like to add ...
I agree with you. I think ...
I'd just like to pick up on one thing you said.
I'm not sure I understood what you said about ...

5 **Follow up by asking each other the following examiner's questions.**

Customer relations

1 A lot of companies say they listen to their customers. Do you think they really do?
2 Which companies in your experience practise good customer relations? Which don't?
3 Do you think technology has helped customer relations or not?

Communication skills

1 Were you ever prepared at school or college for job interviews? Do you think such preparation would help?
2 Apart from an interview what other techniques are used to evaluate job candidates? Do they work?

12.1 Crossing cultures

VOCABULARY

Globalisation

1 Why do you think Kofi Annan said this?

'... arguing against globalisation is like arguing against the laws of gravity.'
Kofi Annan, United Nations

2 Complete the table (sometimes more than one adjective is possible).

Noun	Adjective(s)
1 ____________	social
2 economy	____________
3 competition	____________
4 ____________	growing
5 influence	____________
6 ____________	integrated
7 corporation	____________
8 development	____________

3 What does the term *globalisation* mean to you?

4 Mark the following aspects of globalisation positive (+), negative (-) or don't know (?). Compare and discuss with your partner.

1 free trade (abolition of trade barriers)
2 opening of markets (deregulation of industries like telecoms and energy)
3 social integration and merging of cultures (the global village)
4 increased competition in the world market
5 free movement of labour (migration of workers)
6 free movement of capital
7 development of advanced communications
8 reduction in the cost of goods
9 growing influence of multinational corporations

5 Which of these effects can you see particularly in your country?

READING

Cross-cultural communication

6 **Why is culture important to business people? Discuss with a partner.**

7 **Read this opening passage from a book by Neil Bromford on cross-cultural communication. Choose the best 'blurb' to go on the back of the book.**

CHAPTER ONE

One feature of the global economy and the mobile workforce is that people are coming into contact with other cultures more and more. It's not uncommon for a Spanish manager to be working for an American bank in Shanghai or an English customer to phone a call centre in India that belongs to a German company.

In business, awareness of cultural differences doesn't just mean knowing about the habits of different countries: that Japanese people hate to lose face, that Saudis like to chat and are rarely pressed for time, that Norwegians dislike the use of political influence in business.

Cultural differences may exist between one country and another, but unfamiliar behaviour can just as easily be found between two companies, or two departments, or two social groups, or two generations, or between men and women. A lack of awareness of this fact can seriously undermine your effectiveness in business. This book attempts to …

1

A great insight into the ways that different nationalities like to conduct business. Indispensable reading for all international managers.

2

In this new guide to cross-cultural communication, Neil Bromford highlights the effects of globalisation and its implications for the way we interact with each other.

3

A refreshing look at cross-cultural communication that takes into account the differences that exist not only between national groups but also within companies and society itself.

8 **Think of a title for Neil Bromford's book.**

9 **Look at these words (1–8) from the text above and find a synonym (A–I) for each.**

0 feature	A unusual
1 uncommon	B aspect
2 awareness	C strange
3 to lose face	D knowledge
4 to chat	E to feel humiliated
5 pressed for time	F to weaken
6 influence	G to make conversation
7 unfamiliar	H in a hurry
8 undermine	I power to persuade

READING

1 **Make a list of three *dos* and three *don'ts* for people who have to do business in a different culture.**

2 **Dr A J Schuler gives advice on improving cross-cultural communication in organisations. Read the text and choose the best word (A, B, C or D) to fill each gap.**

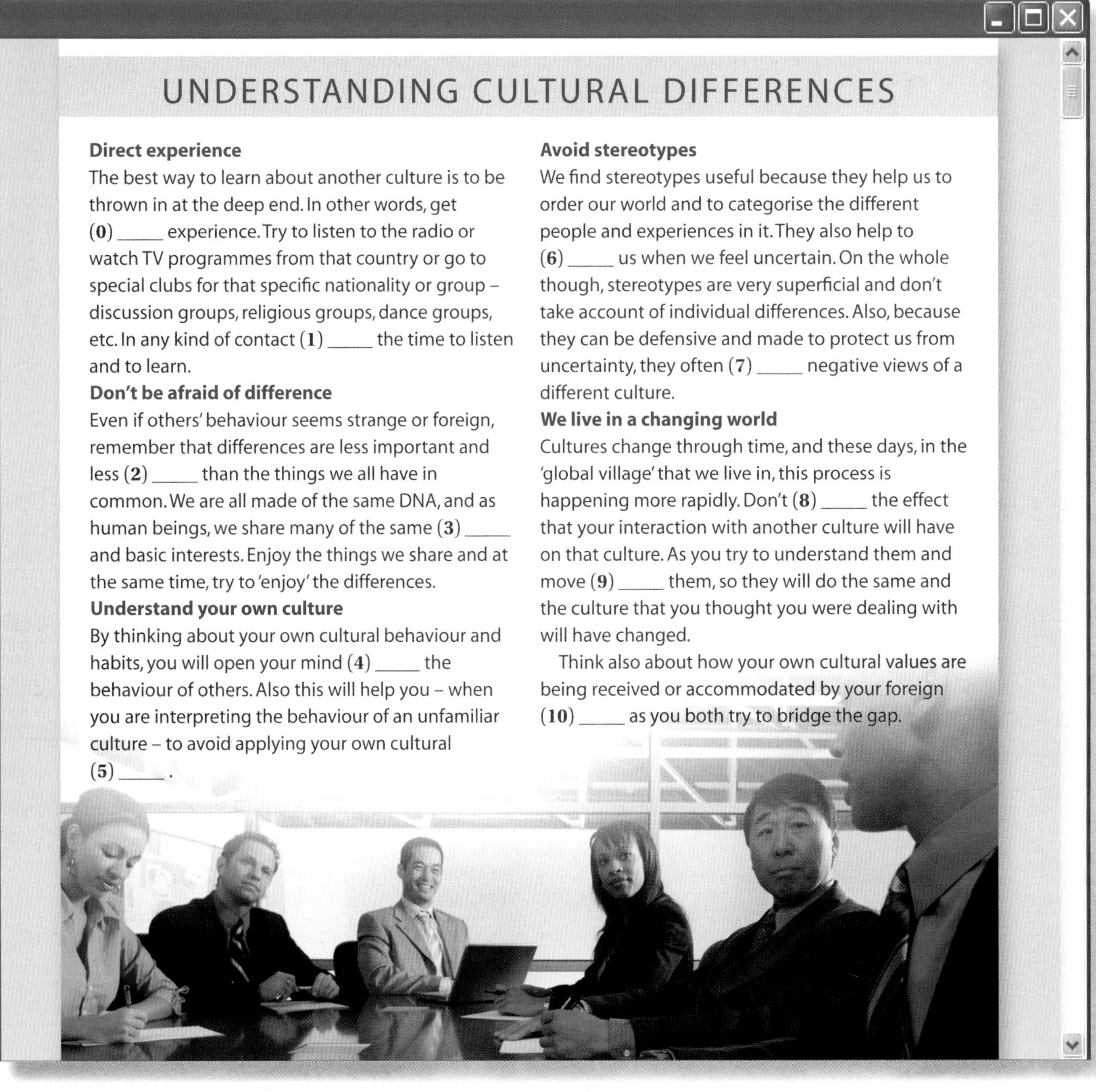

UNDERSTANDING CULTURAL DIFFERENCES

Direct experience

The best way to learn about another culture is to be thrown in at the deep end. In other words, get (**0**) _____ experience. Try to listen to the radio or watch TV programmes from that country or go to special clubs for that specific nationality or group – discussion groups, religious groups, dance groups, etc. In any kind of contact (**1**) _____ the time to listen and to learn.

Don't be afraid of difference

Even if others' behaviour seems strange or foreign, remember that differences are less important and less (**2**) _____ than the things we all have in common. We are all made of the same DNA, and as human beings, we share many of the same (**3**) _____ and basic interests. Enjoy the things we share and at the same time, try to 'enjoy' the differences.

Understand your own culture

By thinking about your own cultural behaviour and habits, you will open your mind (**4**) _____ the behaviour of others. Also this will help you – when you are interpreting the behaviour of an unfamiliar culture – to avoid applying your own cultural (**5**) _____ .

Avoid stereotypes

We find stereotypes useful because they help us to order our world and to categorise the different people and experiences in it. They also help to (**6**) _____ us when we feel uncertain. On the whole though, stereotypes are very superficial and don't take account of individual differences. Also, because they can be defensive and made to protect us from uncertainty, they often (**7**) _____ negative views of a different culture.

We live in a changing world

Cultures change through time, and these days, in the 'global village' that we live in, this process is happening more rapidly. Don't (**8**) _____ the effect that your interaction with another culture will have on that culture. As you try to understand them and move (**9**) _____ them, so they will do the same and the culture that you thought you were dealing with will have changed.

Think also about how your own cultural values are being received or accommodated by your foreign (**10**) _____ as you both try to bridge the gap.

	A	B	C	D
0	A unique	B first-hand	C original	D personnel
1	A take	B have	C spend	D pass
2	A many	B numerous	C ample	D amount
3	A motors	B motivators	C motivations	D motifs
4	A up	B for	C of	D to
5	A standards	B mentality	C figures	D thought
6	A assure	B ensure	C insure	D reassure
7	A make	B promote	C mean	D recommend
8	A undergo	B underprice	C underestimate	D understand
9	A to	B across	C close	D towards
10	A opposite	B counterpart	C relation	D workmate

GRAMMAR

Grammar Tip

All the verb forms in exercise 3 are used to speculate about the past; in other words to wonder how things might have been different from what they actually were.

Speculation

3 What is implied about what actually happened in each of these cases?

0 If I had listened to your advice, I would never have taken the train.
I took the train and it was a disaster.
1 I would be a millionaire by now if I had taken up her offer.
2 If I were braver, I would have told him what I thought.
3 I shouldn't have been so hasty in my judgement of her.
4 I wish we had been taught to speak languages better at school.
5 Without influential political connections, he wouldn't have got so far.
6 He should have thought before he spoke.
7 She could have been anything she wanted to be, if she had put her mind to it.
8 In hindsight, it might have been more polite to arrive a little early.

4 Complete the following sentences

0 I'm glad she spoke good English. It *could have been* (could / be) difficult otherwise.
1 If I had known I was going to have to pay for myself, I ____________________ (never / accept) their invitation.
2 No-one would have heard me say I was leaving if he ____________________ (not / put) the call on speaker phone.
3 I know you didn't want to go to their party, but you ____________________ (should / reply) to the invitation.
4 Never eat raw vegetables – they ____________________ (might / wash) in unclean water.
5 You ____________________ (should / not / take) a gift. No-one else did and I think the hosts were embarrassed.
6 I really wanted to meet Anna – I wish you ____________________ (introduce) me.

5 Study the following culturally sensitive situations. What is the best way to handle each situation?

1 Serge prided himself on his adventurousness with food. Until, that is, Mr Sato, the company's main Japanese supplier, invited him out to dinner and ordered them each a dish consisting of a small charred bird. As Serge hesitated Mr Sato proceeded to eat his bird whole, head and all.
2 Tina was pressed for time. She was at the Milan trade fair only for one day with too many people to see and too many things to do. Her heart sank as she saw Umberto Ginelli approaching. Signor Ginelli was one of her best customers but always seemed to have all the time in the world to chat.
3 Frank was known for telling jokes in poor taste and Stefan was dreading spending another evening with him, especially with his boss there, as he was easily offended. Then Frank began, 'Did you hear the one about the Irishman and the American tourist?'
4 Maison Blanc was a very expensive restaurant and Sarah had always wanted to go there. But now she was there, she couldn't relax. Malcolm had invited everyone in the team to celebrate his promotion, but it wasn't really clear whether he was going to pay or each person had to pay for themselves.

6 Have you had any similar experiences? Describe them to your partner. Ask what they would have done in the same situation.

READING

1 **Work with your partner to answer the following quiz taken from the in-flight magazine *International Business Traveller*.**

CHINA RULES

Doing business in China is now commonplace for many western companies and understanding Chinese business culture is a key to success. How well do you know the rules? Try our quiz and find out.

1 When you first meet your Chinese partner, you should
A shake hands.
B just nod your head.
C bow.

2 Exchanging business cards is
A important.
B unimportant.
C unnecessary (no-one reads them anyway).

3 At the beginning of your discussion
A exchange a little small talk.
B take time to get to know each other.
C get straight to the point.

4 Address your Chinese partner
A by his first name.
B by his surname.
C by his formal title.

5 When attending a business meeting
A dress casually.
B dress formally.
C dress in smart casual clothes.

6 If you are visiting for the first time from a foreign country
A bring a substantial gift.
B bring a small gift.
C avoid giving gifts.

7 When it comes to negotiating terms and prices, bear in mind that
A Chinese people like to haggle.
B most contracts are non-negotiable.
C once agreed, the terms cannot be changed.

8 Mentioning that you know important or influential people is considered
A very useful.
B normal.
C bad taste.

9 At a meal it is normal to propose a toast to
A the leader of the Chinese state.
B the most important person present.
C no-one.

10 You should treat your business partner as
A just a business partner.
B a mentor.
C also a friend.

1A 2A 3B 4C 5B 6B 7A 8B 9B 10C

2 **Compare your answers with the ones given. How did you do? Are you surprised?**

LISTENING

Understanding business culture

3 12.1 **You will hear an extract from the radio series *The real world of business.* In this programme an American electronics entrepreneur talks about his experience of doing business in China. Listen and mark one letter (A, B or C) for the correct answer.**

1 Jim hadn't realised that Guanxi was
  A so vital in business.
  B so common in Chinese culture.
  C such a complicated principle.

2 He defines Guanxi as
  A building a support network of collaborators in business.
  B the exchange of presents between collaborators.
  C the experience you gain from doing business over a long time.

3 A lot of foreign companies
  A use Chinese interpreters.
  B fail because they don't understand Guanxi.
  C try to form partnerships with Chinese business people.

4 The Chinese government's policy on bribery is
  A quite relaxed.
  B much stricter than it used to be.
  C to ignore it.

5 You should show an interest in
  A the most important person in the group.
  B Chinese food.
  C Chinese culture and society.

6 When you receive a business card you should
  A read it properly before putting it away.
  B not put it in your pocket.
  C give yours at the same time.

7 One reason it takes time to get an agreement is
  A the Chinese don't like to commit themselves.
  B there are often many levels of management to go through.
  C they will want to solve all the small problems first.

8 The most important thing is
  A to be patient.
  B to understand the tax laws.
  C to learn some Chinese.

WRITING

A market profile report

4 Following a recent business trip to China to investigate the possibilities of importing teas, your manager has asked you to write a report on the particularities of doing business over there. Write the report, including the following points:

- the aims of your visit.
- how your meetings with tea manufacturers went.
- the reaction of your potential business partners to your proposals.
- advice and recommendations for other colleagues who may follow up this visit.

12.2 Social English

VOCABULARY

Conversation starters

1 Match each statement with a short response.

1 Hi, how are you? (→ D)
2 I'm so sorry to be late.
3 Hello, you must be Mr Channing.
4 Phew, it's freezing today.
5 I'm afraid I'm a bit pressed for time this morning.
6 And this is Colin, my partner.
7 Thank you for finding the time to see me.
8 Hey, I like your new premises.
9 You're looking well.
10 So, how's business?

A Hi there, good to meet you.
B Thank you, so are you.
C Yes, they're a big improvement.
D Very well, thanks. And you?
E Oh, not at all. I've been looking forward to it.
F Busy as ever, but it's going well.
G OK, then we'll get straight down to business.
H Don't worry. It's not a problem.
I Yes, that's right. Good to meet you.
J It is, but at least it's not raining.

LISTENING

Small talk: short responses

2 Work with a partner. How would you respond to these questions? Write your ideas in column 1 (*Response 1*).

Question	Response 1	Response 2
1 How was your trip?	________	________
2 Did you find our offices easily?	________	________
3 Can I get you a coffee before we start?	________	________
4 How are you fixed for time?	________	________
5 Sorry, do you mind if I just take this call?	________	________
6 Are you expecting it to be a good year?	________	________
7 Can I be of any help with the marketing side of things?	________	________
8 Would you like to go for a meal this evening?	________	________
9 Would you like a lift back to the station?	________	________

3 12.2 Listen and note down the responses you hear to each question in column 2 (*Response 2*).

4 Work with your partner. Act out the dialogue again. This time give the opposite response to each question.

SPEAKING

Social situations

5 **You represent a supplier of car heaters from your country. You are interested in supplying your heaters to Jaguar Cars in the UK. As a first meeting, they have arranged a tour of their manufacturing plant. Your host is the production manager.**

- Work with your partner.
- Act out the situation, following the steps.

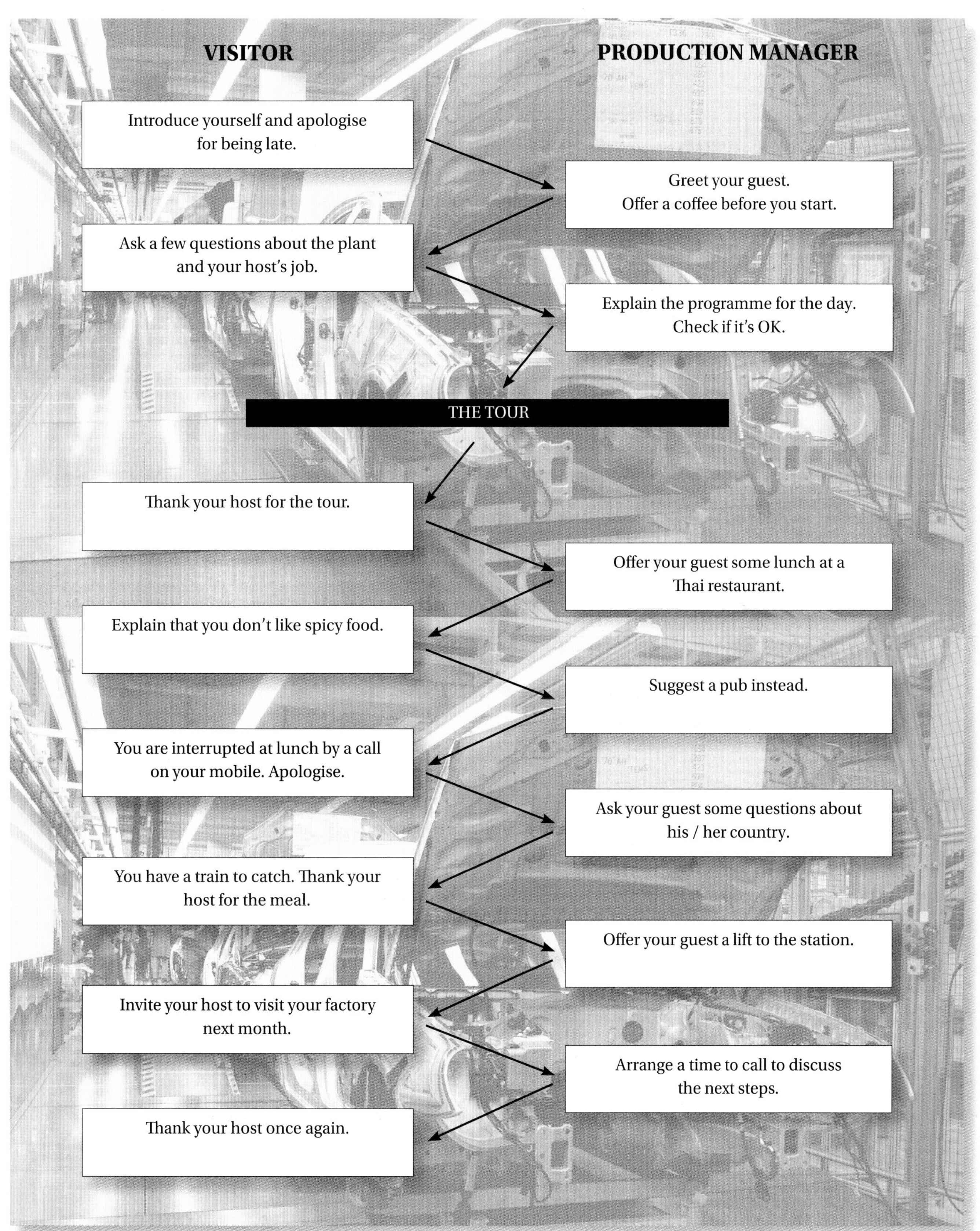

12.3 Reading Test: Part Five and Part Six

EXAM FORMAT

Part Five of the Reading Test consists of a business text approximately 250 words long. It is a gapped text, with ten single words missing. The choice of word to fill each gap is completely up to you. The missing words tend to be small words such as *this, but, not, as, rather*, etc.

Part Six of the Reading Test is a passage (a business letter, short article or piece of publicity) of 150–200 words containing some unnecessary words. Each line of the text (twelve in total) will contain either one unnecessary word or none. The aim is to test your ability to proofread business documents.

Give yourself ten minutes to complete each task.

APPROACH

For Part Five, follow these steps.

- Read the instructions twice and make sure you understand the context of the passage and what you are being asked to do.
- Read the passage through quickly (two minutes) to get the general meaning.
- Re-read to the first gap and look at the whole sentence. What word fits grammatically and in meaning?
- If the right word doesn't come to you quickly and instinctively, move on to the next gap.
- Re-read the passage and fill in any gaps you have missed.

For Part Six, follow these steps.

- Read the instructions twice and make sure you understand the context of the passage and what you are being asked to do.
- Read each sentence, not just each line, before trying to identify an unnecessary word.
- Remember not all lines contain a mistake.
- At the end read the text back, taking account of your corrections, and make sure it makes sense.

KEY SKILL 1

Part Five – Choosing the right word

1 Look at this sentence. Think of a word that fits the gap.

Advances have been made not ________ in cleaner fuels, but also in energy efficiency.
The answer is *only* as in the phrase *not only ... but also.*

2 Choose a word for these sentences. Explain why you chose this word.

1 We need to persuade people to use less energy ________ than building new power plants.
2 There is ________ greater awareness these days of environmental issues.
3 ________ far, the company has sold 20m of the new devices and is hopeful that soon every household will have one.

EXAM PRACTICE

3 **Following the approach described on page 124 do Practice Test Part Five.**

PART FIVE

Questions 1–10

- Read this article about business gifts.
- For each question **1–10**, write one word to fill each gap.
- There is an example at the beginning (**0**).

Permitted business gifts

A business courtesy should not be accepted if the donor expects something (**0**) ...in............. return: he may be attempting to gain an unfair advantage or to influence the employee's judgment. Employees (**1**) .... also avoid a pattern of accepting frequent gifts or business courtesies from the same persons or companies.

Employees may not accept honoraria and may not accept expense reimbursements in excess of $50 from any not-for-profit organisation supported by the Company (other (**2**) .... through the Matching Gift Program).

Examples of permitted gifts and business courtesies:

- A ballpoint pen with a company logo would satisfy the test of being promotional (**3**) .... nature and of nominal value. An inscribed gold wristwatch would be unlikely to be nominal in value and, therefore, would (**4**) .... be acceptable.
- Lunch or dinner invitations to reasonably priced establishments (**5**) .... be permitted if furnished in connection with bona fide business meetings or conferences but, (**6**) .... the meal or entertainment is lavish or frequent, it is not acceptable.
- Accepting a reasonably priced meal, golf outing or sporting event or entertainment ticket in the local area (**7**) .... an occasional basis may be reasonable. Regular invitations or accepting a trip out of the local area to attend a golf outing, sporting event or entertainment event is not.

The Company (**8**) .... pays for work-related transportation, lodging and expenses directly or on a pro-rata basis for combined work and personal trips consistent with the Company's existing travel and entertainment policy. Accepting (**9**) .... offer for an expenses paid trip for pleasure with a customer or supplier is (**10**) .... permitted.

KEY SKILL 2

Part Six – Identifying redundant words

Exam Success

Since it is extra words rather than incorrect words you are looking for, you will find that the same type of mistake comes up again and again in each exam paper.

4 **Find the unnecessary word in each sentence.**

1 It is considered as a social mistake to discuss questions of money too openly.
2 If we answered to every demand for a more personalised service, we would be lost.
3 He was happy with the plan because it gave him no flexibility.
4 Public sector workers, normally the lowest paid, they have had big salary rises.
5 When the cost of supplies is too high because the manufacturer is forced to raise his prices.
6 In recent years employers who have been taking more interest in recruitment.
7 However, the company has completely revised its range of products in the 1990s.
8 It is important to give employees an advice on how best to perform their role.

5 **Use these labels to describe the mistakes in exercise 4.**

A unnecessary relative pronoun	E unnecessary article
B inappropriate negative	F unnecessary auxiliary verb
C repeated subject	G double conjunction
D unnecessary adverb	H extra preposition

6 **Following the approach on page 124 do Practice Test Part Six on page 126.**

EXAM PRACTICE

PART SIX

Questions 1–12

- Read the text below about cross-cultural communication in education.
- In most of the lines there is one extra word. It is either grammatically incorrect or does not fit in with the sense of the text. Some lines, however, are correct.
- If a line is correct, write **CORRECT** next to it.
- If there is an extra word, write **the extra word** next to it.
- There are two examples at the beginning (**0** and **00**).

Communication in the classroom

0 Everything that what happens in a school, and especially in the classroom, WHAT
00 involves communication, the act of sharing information. Sometimes CORRECT
1 communication involves using oral or written symbols. On the other
2 occasions, communication involves various types of non-verbal symbols, including
3 body language. Most behaviour problems in schools, and their resolutions, they
4 involve some type of a communication. Communication permeates education.
5 Communication is culture bound. The way an individual communicates with
6 emanates from his or her culture. Of course, a person may know more than
7 one culture or may be have competent in a combination of cultures.
8 Nonetheless, one basic truth prevails: when communication is a product of culture.
9 Students with different cultural norms are at risk if teachers have a little
10 knowledge, sensitivity or appreciation of the diversity in communication
11 styles. Such teachers may not perceive differences as problems and respond to
12 students' diversity with negative attitudes, low expectations and culturally
inappropriate teaching and assessment procedures.

MODULE 2

Page 22, Exercise 3

Student B

Company name:	Bustwell's
Company type:	Limited company, equal shares owned by two directors
Date established:	1952
Turnover:	£88 million per year
Number of employees:	220
Main products:	toys, cameras and photographic equipment, electrical goods and kitchenware
Locations:	five large department stores in city centres in the south east of England

Brief history:

1952 – opens as haberdasher's and kitchenware shop in London
1960s – develops into department store, opens toy department
1970s – six new stores in other cities in south-east
1980s – moves into furniture and household goods
1995 – gives up furniture – strong competition
2002 – new financial management; closes stores in two locations
2004 – concentrates more on toys, photographic and electrical
2006 – loss in first half of year

Core competencies:	retailing; photographic expertise
Financial situation:	profits in decline; small amount of debt; owns three shop premises; others on long leases
Market prospects:	difficult; competition from out-of-town stores
Market price:	could be a bargain

MODULE 4

Page 37, Exercise 6

Zig Ziglar's closing the sale

'Every sale has five basic obstacles: no need, no money, no hurry, no desire, no trust.'

Secrets of Closing the Sale, Zig Ziglar

MODULE 6

Page 57, Exercise 7

Shall we do business?

If you answered mostly A: You want to co-operate at all times with your suppliers. But be careful: not everyone in business is as nice and trusting as you are.

If you answered mostly B: You are a principled person who looks for the win–win situation in deals.

If you answered mostly C: You're a tough customer! There are no such things as friends for you in business, especially among your suppliers.

BEC HIGHER EXAM: KEY INFORMATION

EXAM AIMS

Each BEC examination is 'an internationally recognised business qualification that can show that you have learned English to an appropriate standard and can use it in a professional context.' It is increasingly recognised by both companies and organisers of higher education courses in business.

Success at BEC Higher shows a prospective employer not only that you have a high level of English, but also that you have the communication skills to perform a number of business tasks in English: presenting, participating in meetings, writing letters and reports, and reading business articles, reports and correspondence. Knowledge of these skills is an important element of the exam.

LEVEL

Where BEC Higher stands in relation to other exams and indicators:

Traditional Description	Council of Europe Level	Cambridge General English	TOEIC	Cambridge BEC
Expert	C2+		900	
Proficient	C2	CPE	750	
Advanced	C1	CAE		BEC Higher
Upper intermediate	B2+	FCE	600	BEC Vantage
	B2			
Intermediate	B1+	PET	450	BEC Preliminary
	B1			
Pre-intermediate	A2+	KET		
Elementary	A2			
Beginner	A1			

CONTENT

The BEC Higher exam tests all four skills: Reading, Writing, Listening and Speaking.

Paper	Parts	Time	Details
Reading	6 parts	1 hour	Approximately 2100 words in total; 52 questions in total
Writing	2 tasks (from 4 questions)	1 hour 10 minutes	(1) 130 word report (2) 200–250 word letter, proposal or report
Listening	3 parts	about 40 minutes including 10 mins transfer time	30 questions / items
Speaking	3 parts	16 minutes	2 examiners, 2 candidates (occasionally 2:3 format)

It also tests, as mentioned above, your ability to operate effectively in a range of business tasks. The main examples of these are:

- presenting and talking about yourself
- presenting and describing a company and its organisation
- taking part in business discussions: arguing a case, making recommendations, etc
- speaking on the telephone
- giving opinions on a range of business issues, such as: marketing, cost control, human resources issues, management, distribution, environmental issues, etc
- presenting facts and figures and describing trends
- ordering and receiving orders for services
- dealing with customers (orders, problems, complaints)

These are *Can-do* statements describing the abilities of successful BEC Higher candidates (from the Council of Europe's ALTE project).

Listening / Speaking

- Can ask questions outside own immediate area of work.
- Can argue her/his case effectively or discuss against a case.
- Can talk about most aspects of her/his work.

Reading

- Can understand most articles likely to be encountered during the course of her/his work including complex ideas expressed in complex language.

Writing

- Can handle a wide range of situations in which professional services are requested from colleagues or external contacts.
- Can write any type of letter necessary in the course of her/his work.

MARKS

Your overall grade is based on the total score gained in all papers. You don't have to 'pass' each paper in order to pass the examination. There are three pass grades: A, B and C and two fail grades: D and E. To get a C grade you typically need about 60% of the total marks.

You will receive a statement of your results showing your performance in each skill on the following scale: Exceptional – Good – Borderline – Weak.

Each paper carries 25% of the marks. The marking criteria are as follows:

Reading and Listening

All answers carry one mark and are either right or wrong, with one mark available for each. Spelling (British or American) should be correct.

Writing

Answers are judged on: realisation of the task (ie answering the question); accurate use of language; range of structure and vocabulary; organisation; appropriate tone and format.

Speaking

Your speaking is judged on: overall performance; ability to interact; organisation of discourse; grammar and vocabulary; pronunciation.

FAQS

1 How long will I have to wait for my results? Usually about 7 weeks
2 How much do I have to know about business? Even if you do not have much work experience yet, you should be able to express opinions on basic issues like customer relations, controlling costs, taking risks, managing people, etc.
3 Is spelling important? Yes. Both in the Writing Paper and in the Listening Paper, incorrect spelling will be penalised.
4 In Speaking Test Part Two, does each candidate get the same list of subjects to talk about? No, each person in the pair is given a different list.
5 What is the ten minute 'transfer time' in the Listening Paper? It's the time given at the end to transfer your answers to an answer sheet to be read by computer.
6 Will I also have transfer time in the Reading Paper? No. It is included in the one hour. We recommend that you transfer the answers at the end of each section.
7 2000 words in an hour is a lot of reading. How can I get faster at reading? Just keep reading as much as you can – magazines, articles, business books.
8 What one piece of advice would you give me for the exam? In the Speaking and Writing Papers, act as if the tasks were real work tasks.

EXAM DATES

There are regular dates (approximately eight) through the year. The exam dates for paper-based BEC and computer-based BEC are available on the Cambridge ESOL website (www.CambridgeESOL.org).

Speaking

Presenting facts

OK. If everyone is ready, I'll begin. / Shall we begin? / Shall we get started?
I'm going to describe / present / explain / give you some information about ...
I'd like to say a few words about ...
Please interrupt me if there's something that's not clear.
Please leave your questions until the end and I'll (do my best to) answer them then.

I'd like to begin by saying / describing / explaining ...
So why should we ...?
There are two / three / four key points to note about ...
Firstly ... Secondly ... And finally ...
It's also worth noting that ...

So, I think I've covered the main points.
So, to sum up, ...
So, are there any questions?
So, if there aren't any more questions, I'll end there. Thanks for your attention.

Asking the presenter questions

Thank you. That was a very interesting talk.
You mentioned ... Why / What / How ...?
I'd just like to pick up on one thing you said ...
You used the term ... What exactly did you mean by that?
I'm not sure I understood what you said about ...
When you talked about ...., did you mean that ...?
I was a little surprised that you said ... because, for me, ...

Giving personal information

I don't have much time for hobbies, but ...
I like eating out, spending time with friends, ...
I hope to get a job as a ...
I plan to enter a company at managerial level.
Most people go on to work in ...

Describing your organisation

It's a large / medium-sized / small business.
It's a state-owned / private / family company.
We provide ... services to the ... industry.
We make / sell / distribute ... / We advise ... on ...
We do research into ... / We work with ...

Business is booming / thriving / steady / reasonable / slow / tough.

Our main customers are ...

It's quite relaxed / informal / people-friendly / traditional / formal / dynamic / forward-looking

Describing your job / course

I work as a junior / middle manager / a trainee / an apprentice.
I work in the sales / purchasing / finance / HR department.

My job involves ...-*ing*.
I'm responsible for ... / I'm in charge of ...
I have to (make sure that) ... / I deal with ...
There are six of us in the department.
I report to the ... manager. / I work with ...

It's a challenging / demanding / rewarding / satisfying / fairly routine / uneventful job.
It's sponsored by a pharmaceutical company.
It offers very practical training in ...
It's a kind of MBA.

Stating preferences

Personally I'd go for / favour option A because it's ...
I think option A has much more going for it. For a start ...
My preference would be option A, because ...

I'm not so keen on option B.
I have several reservations about option B. Firstly, it's ...
I think option B has several drawbacks. It's ...
Option B, on the other hand, is too ...
We shouldn't choose option B just because ...

I'd rather go for option A than B.
I'd much prefer to choose A than B.
We would be better off choosing A, because ...
All in all, option A represents the best solution because ...

Both options have their pros and cons.
There's not much to choose between them.

Expressing opinions

What do you think about this idea? / How do you feel about this idea?
Personally, I think it's ...
In my opinion ... / For me, it's ...
On the whole, it seems ...
I'm not sure: on the one hand ...

Do you think it will work?
I'm sure it will.
I certainly hope so.
I doubt it. / Not really. / It's unlikely to.
It might do. / Perhaps.
Who knows? / Your guess is as good as mine.
I think it's risky.
You're right, it is. / I agree with you.
It is risky, but ...
Maybe so, but ...
I don't see it that way. For me, ...

Discussing options and making recommendations

So, we've been asked to ...
So, we're here to ...
I suggest that we (do) ...
I think we ought to (do) ...
I'd recommend (doing) ...
For me, the best thing would be to ...

Another option would be to ...
We could try (doing) ...
Instead of (doing) ..., we could (do) ...
If we were to (do) ..., then we could (do) ...

The advantage of that would be ...
In that way we would ...

What do you think / suggest?
What's your opinion / view?
I agree with you.
I think that's an excellent idea.
I see what you're saying, but wouldn't it be better to ...

I think that might be quite difficult / dangerous / expensive.

Telephoning

You hear	You can respond
Hello. Can I help you?	Yes. I'm calling about ... Can I speak to Mr ...? I'm trying to get in touch with ... Can I speak to the person who deals with ...?
One moment, I'll put you through. / I'll see if he's free.	Thank you.
I'm just going to put you on hold for a moment.	OK.
I'm afraid he's not available. Would you like to hold?	That's OK. I'll call back later. / No, but could you tell him I called.
Can I take a message?	Yes, just tell her ...
Can you ask Sarah to arrive fifteen minutes earlier?	Sure, I'll see she gets the message.
Can you tell me the price of a ...?	One moment, I'll just check.
I'll have to get back to you on that.	OK. If you can call me soon, I'd appreciate it.
Is John there?	Yes, I'll just get him for you.
I'll see you in the bar.	Great. See you there.

Chairing a meeting

OK. Shall we start?
As you know, we're here to discuss / talk about / consider ...
The aim of this meeting is to ...
Carlos, would you like to begin?

We're running short of time. I think we should move on to the next point.
I think we're straying off the subject. / I think that's a discussion for another meeting.
Perhaps we can come back to this later.
Can I just interrupt you, Julia?

So, to sum up, we've agreed that ...
Does anyone have anything further to add?
OK. Let's leave it there. Thank you all for your input.

Negotiating

Let me just outline our position.
Let me just explain what we're looking for.

In exchange, we can offer ...
This would benefit you in two ways: Firstly, ...

That would be very difficult for us.
I would need to speak to my manager before agreeing anything.
I'd like to give that some thought before giving you a definite answer.
Would you be prepared to offer us a discount?
Can you move on the price at all?
If we were to ..., would you be willing to ...?
Try to look at it from our perspective. / Put yourself in our shoes.

In principle, that sounds fine.
I think that sounds fair.

Just to recap what we've agreed ...

Structuring a discussion

So we're here to discuss ... and there are two issues we need to look at:

- Firstly, ...
- And secondly ...

Let's look at the first issue. How can we ...?
Well, for me the best way is ...
I agree but there's one point I'd like to add ...
I think that's one possibility. Another would be to ...
So, just to sum up, we've agreed that we should ...

Giving a mini-presentation

So why should we ...?
I think there are three important points here.
Firstly, ... Secondly, ... And finally, ...

I'd like to say a few words about ...
Of course, it's important to ...
But on the other hand, ...
There is also the question of ...

I think I've covered the main points ...
Those are my views on it ...
What do you think ...?
Do you agree ...?

Yes. There's just one point I'd like to add ...
I agree with you. I think ...
I'd just like to pick up on one thing you said.
I'm not sure I understood what you said about ...

Everyday phrases

You hear	You can respond
Hi, how are you?	Very well thanks. And you?
Hello, I'm Sajid.	Good / Pleased to meet you, Sajid. My name's Paul.
I'm so sorry to be late.	Don't worry. / No problem.
Thank you for your help.	Not at all. My pleasure.
Would you like a coffee?	Thanks. I'd love one.
Can I give you a lift to the station?	That's very kind of you, but I don't want to put you out.
How was your trip?	Not bad, thanks. The plane wasn't delayed / was on time.
How are you fixed for time?	I have to catch a train at 3pm.
Sorry, do you mind if I just take this call?	No, please go ahead.
Do you expect to come back in the summer?	I hope so. / I expect so. / No, I doubt it.
Would you like to go for a meal this evening?	That would be very nice. / I'd love to, but I can't.
I'm afraid I can't make it to the meeting.	Oh, that's a shame / pity. / I'm sorry to hear that.
Actually I think that's my pen.	I'm so sorry. I didn't realise.

Writing

Comparing two graphs

The two graphs show / illustrate the development of ... over the period ... to ...
If we look at the first graph, we can see ...
From the first graph, we can see ...
... a steady increase in sales of about ... %.
... that sales increased steadily by 2%.
... there was a significant increase / rise in sales.
... there was a general decline / fall / decrease / drop in sales.
... with some variations / fluctuations.

Sales peaked / reached a low point in ...
Sales remained stable / fluctuated / went up and down.
Following the slump in 2004, sales recovered / picked up.
Over the same period, supply of ... failed to keep pace with demand.

The reason for this was probably ...
This seems to have been due to ...
This can probably be explained by ...

The relation between the two sets of figures is clear.
These two developments are clearly linked.
These figures suggest that ...
The conclusion to draw from this data is that ...

Letters

Beginning and ending

Dear Sir / Madam	Yours faithfully
Dear Ms Johnson	Yours sincerely
Dear David	Kind regards

Reason for writing

I am writing to apologise for / enquire about / thank you for / express our dissatisfaction with ...
I am writing in answer to your letter / advertisement / enquiry about ...
Following our recent meeting / telephone conversation, I am writing to ...
I was given your name by ..., who suggested you might be able to help us to ...

The background

As you may know, Gimbles Ltd is an electronics manufacturer based in ...
As you will recall, three weeks ago we ...
Recently, we ...

The result

As a result of this, we have had to ...
Consequently, we would like to ...
The result of this is that ...

The next step

What I propose is that ...
In order to resolve this matter, I suggest that ...
We would appreciate it if you could ...
We would be grateful if you could now ...

Further communication

Please do not hesitate to contact me / us if you wish to discuss any of the above.
I look forward to hearing from you / receiving ...

Signing off

Thank you again for your custom / interest / understanding.
Once again, my apologies for the delay / misunderstanding / error.
I hope you find this solution satisfactory.

Reports and proposals

This report sets out / presents the findings of the ... committee into ...
The purpose of this report is to analyse / describe / clarify the current situation with ...
This proposal has been prepared in response to a demand from ... for ...
In response to a request from ... for ..., we would like to submit the following proposal.

The scope of our study was ...
We studied / examined ...
What we found was that ...
Our main findings were as follows: ...

The reasons for this situation seem to be ...
This can be attributed to (the fact that) ...
There are two factors that have contributed to this: ...

The advantages of this approach would be firstly ...
This approach would have two benefits. Firstly, ...
The drawbacks would be ...
The only disadvantage we can envisage is ...

Our conclusions are that ...
In conclusion, we would like to propose that / recommend that ...
Your comments on the above report / proposals would be very welcome. Please reply to ... @ ...

Linking words

But

Although it is expensive, it's worth investing in.
In spite of / Despite the high cost, it's worth investing in.
It is expensive. **Nevertheless**, it's worth investing in.

Domestic sales have been slow, **whereas** exports have been booming.
Domestic sales have been slow. **However**, exports have been booming.
Domestic sales have been slow. Exports, **on the other hand**, have been booming.
Domestic sales have been slow. Exports, **by contrast**, have been booming.

And

As well as having good qualifications, she also has lots of experience.
Besides having good qualifications, she also has lots of experience.
She has good qualifications. **In addition / Moreover / Furthermore**, she has lots of experience.

So

Because tomorrow is a public holiday, the office will be closed.
Tomorrow is a public holiday. **Consequently**, the office will be closed.
Tomorrow is a public holiday. **As a result**, the office will be closed.
The office will be closed tomorrow **because of** the public holiday.
The office will be closed tomorrow **owing to** the public holiday.
The office will be closed tomorrow **on account of** the public holiday.

Then

They investigated the matter thoroughly. **Then** they published their findings.

After investigating the matter thoroughly, they published their findings.
When they had investigated the matter thoroughly, they published their findings.
Following a thorough investigation of the matter, they published their findings.

Telephoning

Sorry, I got cut off Sorry, the line was disconnected
Can you speak up? Can you speak more loudly?
I'm a bit tied up at the moment I'm a bit busy / not available at the moment
Sorry, I didn't catch that Sorry, I didn't hear that
Can you just hold on a moment? Can you please wait?

Timing

be on schedule be as planned
be behind / ahead of schedule be later / earlier than planned
It arrived just in time It arrived before it was too late
Sorry to ask you at such short notice Sorry to give you so little time to prepare
It's better late than never It's better to have some outcome, however delayed, than none at all
in the long run in the long term
a short-sighted view only seeing the immediate benefits

Problems and solutions

tackle / address the problem deal with the problem
find a stop-gap solution find a temporary solution
kill two birds with one stone solve two problems at once
cut corners reach a solution, usually quickly or easily, often by not observing correct practice
nip it in the bud stop a problem before it gets worse
teething problems problems always encountered in the early stages of a project

Action

I think we should go for it Let's do it
Let's get down to business Let's begin
There's no point in beating about the bush There's no point in not coming to the main point
We need to take the bull by the horns We need to address the issue
Actions speak louder than words What somebody does shows more than what they say they will do

Understanding

I'm not with you / I didn't follow you I didn't understand
I couldn't make head or tail of it I couldn't understand it at all
His presentation went right over my head His presentation was too difficult to understand
I don't have a clue what you're talking about I don't know what you're talking about
You'll get the hang of it You'll learn how it works

Decisions

I'm in two minds about it I can't make up my mind about it
It's up to you It's your decision
She's sitting on the fence She's not committing herself to one side or another
We need to bite the bullet We need to take a decision, even if it's risky
We can't put it off any longer We can't delay making a decision

Making predictions

It's a foregone conclusion The result is obvious
It's all up in the air There's no saying what will happen
They're bound to refuse They're certain to refuse
I'll bet that ... I can be sure that ...

Negotiating

The bottom line for us is ... What we fundamentally need and want is ...
put yourself in our shoes see it from our perspective
put your cards on the table be open and frank
find common ground find points where we agree
a stumbling block / sticking point a point where we can't agree
You drive a hard bargain You demand a lot

Discussion

Let's not split hairs Let's not debate unimportant details
I'd like to take issue with I'm going to argue against / debate
That's beside the point That's not relevant
Let's try to keep an open mind Let's not make a judgement too quickly
Let's not jump to conclusions Let's not make a judgement too quickly

Miscellaneous

It's not really my cup of tea It's not something I like
10% increase in real terms (financial) 10% increase, taking into account inflation
She's got everything in hand She's organised everything
I'm snowed under I have far too much work
We're going round in circles We're not making any progress
make a breakthrough make a big step forward
go back to the drawing board start again

Module 1

 1.1 The future of human resources *(page 9)*

1 I think the problem is that in the last fifteen years, employers haven't shown their employees much loyalty. They've hired and fired pretty much at will, according to whether the market dictated that they needed to increase or reduce the workforce. The flipside of this is that employees now, particularly those in the 25 to 35 age group, don't feel much loyalty to their employer either. Developing strategies to hold on to highly skilled and highly qualified people has become the number one priority in human resources - in all big companies in fact.

2 There's no doubt that in the next ten years there will be a move away from the nine to five office-based model of work. In fact, it's already happening with women, who often find it challenging to balance work and domestic schedules. This could mean more 'teleworking', in other words working at home and being linked to the office by computer; or it could mean shorter working weeks or just more flexible hours. Unless companies offer these possibilities, a lot of people will look for alternative types of work.

3 Companies are finding that graduates and school leavers aren't well enough prepared for working life. This is going to drive two changes, I think. One is a greater co-operation between companies and universities or colleges to ensure that at entry level to the company, people have the right skills. We'll also see more investment in corporate training - corporate universities and so on - so that employees' skills can be moulded to the needs of the company.

4 As the birth rate decreases and life expectancy increases, there will be shortages in the job market. Consequently, a lot of ex-employees who thought they had finished their careers at 60 or whatever, will be called back to work. This will suit the companies, but it will suit the employees too, because their pensions will probably be inadequate to fund their longer retirement.

5 At the moment people in their 50s and 60s are, on the whole, very poorly valued in companies. Firms want to recruit younger employees who are cheaper to employ and are more adaptable to a changing business environment. But as the supply of these younger workers dries up, we'll have to consider older staff differently. I hope that in future the wisdom and experience of this group will become more valued.

 1.2 An environmental accident *(page 12)*

J = Journalist **S** = Spokesperson

J So, can you tell me how this happened?

S Well, it was a very unfortunate combination of events. As you know, weather conditions have been severe in the eastern Atlantic for the last couple of days. The ship's captain reported that the ship was in trouble at 11pm last night and was ordered to make for port as quickly as possible. At 2.30am he reported that she was grounded on some rocks just off the Cornish coast.

J But this isn't the first time this particular ship has been in an accident, is it?

S She has been involved in two incidents in the past, but these had nothing to do with her sea-worthiness. She is a well-maintained ship in excellent working order with an experienced crew on board.

J And what are you intending to do to limit the damage to the environment now?

S Unfortunately, while conditions remain so hostile, there is very little we can do, but the moment the storms subside we will be mounting an operation to transfer the oil off the ship using tugs.

J Do you think that this kind of accident is acceptable?

S I think it needs to be put into perspective. Accidents at sea are far less common than rail or road accidents. The problem is that they attract much more publicity ...

J Well, yes. Whichever way you look at it, it's a PR disaster for your company, isn't it?

S As I've said, this type of incident does attract a lot of media attention. I just hope that the public can see ...

Module 2

 2.1 The PeopleSoft takeover *(page 20)*

Commentator I think you could sum up PeopleSoft's approach to their employees like this: 'We want you to be happy, we want you to do the things you're good at and that you enjoy doing.' Very few big IT consulting companies are like that. They usually throw people straight in at the deep end: put them on jobs where they don't necessarily have much skill or experience, arguing that it's good for them to learn. But I think that although they talked a lot about caring for their people and having fun, PeopleSoft put a lot of responsibility on them too. Like they were saying, 'Here's a job you can do and will enjoy doing, but you'll be accountable for the results'. To enforce that they generally started people on low salaries - and I mean low - and explained that greater rewards would come in time. In fairness, it was direct and honest. In December 2004, when Oracle took over, a lot of employees decided to leave. For a start, the feeling was that their applications just weren't as good as PeopleSoft's - in fact they were probably just more difficult to use - and secondly people thought that Oracle didn't respect employees as much. The CEO of PeopleSoft, Dave Duffield, had a very paternalistic approach - he used to sign his emails 'DAD' (which were his initials). It wasn't well-paid work but people felt valued, which is often more important. Also there was a relaxed atmosphere around the company. The moment the merger was announced, that kind of evaporated. It seemed to become tense, people wondering if the new CEO was going to live up to his reputation for wielding the axe. And, in retrospect, you would have to say they were they right to be worried!

Industry analyst Oracle gets a lot of flak because of its aggressive growth strategy, but I'm afraid in this sector only the big guys are going to survive. The merger with PeopleSoft was a business necessity. It didn't happen because the two companies were so alike - their cultures were very different. At Oracle there's a greater sense of urgency ... it's a stressful environment, but the rewards are huge. I know some reps there who are making millions of dollars. Sure, if you don't cut it, you're toast pretty fast, but that's business. It's survival of the fittest. The differences really come from the nature of the two businesses. Oracle's core product is databases and with databases the customer often makes a decision whether to buy or not in a matter of weeks. With ERP applications, which is more PeopleSoft territory, you can be in discussions with customers for months, analysing their needs and then proposing the right solution before a sale is agreed. So that naturally makes for a different culture. The other thing is that the merger happened really quickly - like marrying before you've really got to know the bride. So, of course people are uncertain. I think in the end, though, as both sets of employees adapt to each other's way of working, things will settle down.

 2.2 Falling shares *(page 22)*

CEO OK, hi everyone. I'll make this brief, because I have another meeting to get to, but what I have to say is no less important for being short.

As you know, in our three-year plan we had a target of 20% growth by the end of this year. As things stand, we're going to be quite a bit short of that – trading circumstances haven't been easy. And unless we do something about it in the next few months, the consequences on our share price could be pretty significant. The markets are already getting a bit twitchy as you will have read in the financial press.

It's unrealistic to think that we are going to trade our way out of this. All the indications are that the market is going to remain flat for at least the next twelve months. So, what I need you to do is to come up with some possible targets for acquisition. We're looking for a medium-sized business, reasonably well established in the market. It doesn't have to be a toy business, but it must be related ... in other words in the leisure retail sector, because that is where our expertise is. I don't need to tell you your jobs, I know you'll be discreet, but do get on with it – time's not on our side. I'll schedule a meeting for a month's time to hear what you've come up with.

Module 3

 3.1 Dealing with problems *(page 30)*

CCO = Call centre operator **C** = Customer

CCO Hello, Penco Telecommunications.

C At last, I was just about to hang up. I've been on the phone for ten minutes going through various options ... none of which I wanted.

CCO I do apologise for the wait, sir. How can I help you?

C I've been waiting in all day for an engineer to come and repair my line. He was due to come at ten o'clock this morning ... it's now three in the afternoon. I telephoned at twelve o'clock and one of your operators promised to call me back, but she hasn't. I've wasted my day waiting around and worse than that I still can't receive any calls.

CCO I'm very sorry. Can I have your number and I'll look into it straightaway?

C Yes, it's 01889 245624.

CCO OK. One moment – I'm going to see who the engineer is that has been assigned to the job ... OK, I have his number. I'm going to put you on hold and try to find out what's happened.

C Please don't disappear. As I said, it took me ten minutes to get through in the first place.

CCO Don't worry, I'll come straight back to you. One moment ... Right, I'm afraid he has been delayed on another job. He apologises for not calling you sooner. He normally works until 5pm but he's offered to work later this evening to fit in your job. He can be there by 6pm. Would that be convenient?

C No, it would not. I'm going out to the cinema this evening.

CCO I quite understand. In that case, I'm going to have to reschedule him for another day. Can you tell me when would be convenient?

C Well, first thing tomorrow morning, but ...

CCO I'll see what I can do. Please just bear with me for a moment while I speak to him again ... right that's arranged for tomorrow morning at nine.

C That's all very well, but what am I supposed to do in the meantime?

CCO Do you have a mobile phone, sir?

C Yes.

CCO What I can do is to divert any calls coming into your office number on to your mobile phone until your line is repaired. Would that be acceptable to you?

C I suppose so. When can you do that?

CCO If you'd like to tell me your mobile number, I can get that activated immediately.

C OK, the number is ...

 3.2 Exam spotlight, Exam practice *(page 35)*

I imagine most of you are here today because you want to find out more about the job of a coach. Some of you will be sceptical about its benefits, others will have already started making a career out of coaching.

I myself have been a coach since the late 90s, but our academy was set up more recently in 2004 in response to a demand for more formal training in the field. We are a private institution and don't rely on any government funding. Our aim was to try to professionalise an industry which until then had been, in this country at any rate, rather disorganised and unregulated. We now have over 450 members and run twelve courses a year in various types of coaching. These range from day seminars for people who are already practising as coaches to four-week courses for the beginner.

So what is a coach exactly? Well, there are many different types of coach offering help in many different aspects of business and personal life: from financial or management coaching through to parent coaching and work-life balance coaching. But the basic principles remain the same whatever the field: using simple psychology and simple direction to help people to believe in themselves and to achieve their goals.

The great thing about coaches is that not only do they help you to identify your goals and the obstacles to achieving them, but they stay there cheering you on from the sidelines. In other words, they always help the client to look forward. This is very unlike traditional counselling, which tends to focus more on past events and mistakes and helping the person to get over these before they can move on.

I'm going to show you a short film of a coaching session in a moment, but before I do, I will just mention something about the rewards of the job, and the qualifications and resources that you need for it because these are questions that will be concerning many of you.

The rewards: well, job satisfaction is, of course, very high. I mean, how often do you come home from work and are able to say, 'Wow, I really made a difference to someone's life today'? As to financial rewards, sessions with coaches usually start at about £70 per hour but experienced coaches can earn anything up to £400 per hour. As to qualifications, you will need to follow an accredited coaching course, such as the ones we run here at the academy, and also you will need considerable experience in the field that you are coaching in. If you don't have this background it will be difficult for the client to have confidence in you.

What else do you need to set up as a coach? Most coaching is done at the client's office or home, but some coaches also see people at their own homes. In fact there's no need always to meet face-to-face. I know of several coaches who conduct sessions by phone or online, even sometimes by text message ...

Module 4

 4.1 Sales techniques *(page 37)*

Sarah We make financial software for medium-sized companies. Competition is strong – not necessarily price competition, because in our sector, quality, reliability and service are far more important factors. We use a sales technique that's called 'relationship selling.' In other words, we spend a lot of time getting to know each prospect's individual needs: their business processes, their strategic aims, and um ... also the issues and constraints they face. The idea is that the customer sees us as a partner, someone who's going to work with them and help them find the best solution for their business. Working this way, there are times when I have to freely admit to people that our products may not be best suited to their particular needs, but to be honest I'd much prefer to be doing that than using some hard-sell technique to push something I don't really believe in myself, you know ...

Presenter Thank you, Sarah. Now, Dale Freidman, I know you have a very different approach ...

Dale I would say so, yes. In my line of business, it's all about perceived benefits – there are some tangible ones like, for example, use of natural ingredients in our deodorants, but everyone in the industry copies ideas, so it's difficult to sustain any kind of technical competitive advantage for long. So, I use a lot of anecdotes when I sell; I tell stories, get people laughing. My approach is direct – I guess some might say pushy, but I get results. I deal only with the decision maker, who's generally a buyer for a chain of stores. You'd be amazed how much time people waste talking to the wrong guy. I always start by presenting them with the most expensive options, because this increases our average sales, and as soon as I get a buying signal from them – it could be anything, you know, just a question like 'What's your most popular product?' – I move in and close the sale by discussing quantities required, special delivery arrangements, favourable payment terms, things that make them feel they're getting added value ...

 4.2 A sales forecast *(page 42)*

Anke Reigl Is everyone ready? Good, then I'll begin. OK ... Well, based on average growth in sales over the last two years and given the relatively stable state of the market at the moment as far as competition is concerned, we're forecasting a fairly modest increase in the first quarter, about 2 to 3%. We expect this to rise to between 7 and 10% in the second and third quarters, after the launch of the new slow-release version of the drug. Marketing tells me – thanks, Werner for your help with this ...

Werner You're welcome.

Anke Reigl ... that demand for this version is strong and should be reflected in sales more or less immediately. So that's the basic picture. There are just a couple of monthly variations to this trend which I'll explain now.

If you look at the graph, you'll see that in March last year sales went up quite sharply and that the figure predicted for this year is much lower. The reason for this is that Bayer had distribution problems and weren't able to supply the required quantities to their customers. We were fortunate, because we were carrying extra stock and were able to take advantage of the situation. I think it's worth noting that disruptions in the supply chain can affect anyone and it really does pay for us to hold a reasonable amount of stock in reserve for events like these.

As you know, sales generally decline in April and May – it's just a seasonal factor – but as I already mentioned, the launch of the new version this year is expected to boost them considerably, especially in April directly after the campaign. They'll drop back a little after that, but in July we'll have the usual early summer phenomenon when distributors ...

Module 5

 5.1 A culture of debt *(page 47)*

Economist Perhaps the greatest legacy of Federal Reserve Chairman Alan Greenspan is the way he transformed people's attitude to credit and debt. During his term of office not only the national debt of America, but also personal debt, increased substantially.

Since the Great Depression of the 1930s, people in America have been naturally reluctant to borrow money. But for this generation, in the US and increasingly globally, debt has become respectable. From an early age, young people take out loans to pay their way through college and borrowing against equity in real estate is now at record levels. Re-mortgaging your home was unheard of generations ago: a second mortgage was an indication of a household in trouble. But today it is routine.

All this is possible because credit is easy and interest rates are low. Banks are encouraged to lend, and often do so irresponsibly. In some states it's possible to get a 100% mortgage – in other words with no down-payment – equivalent to four times a couple's combined annual salary. The market is constantly coming up with new financial products and new ways of extending credit to ordinary people. General Motors, whose automotive business is in decline, now sells home equity loans though a subsidiary: it's the only part of the company that has been consistently profitable in recent years.

The reason for this boom in money lending is clear – to fund consumer spending. As long as people are spending, economic growth continues. In other more conservative borrowing cultures, like Germany, economic growth has slowed because in times of uncertainty people tend to save their money, rather than borrowing and spending to make themselves feel better.

So does the accumulating debt matter? Some say that as long as asset values rise faster than debt, there's no problem. In 2005 Americans were twelve trillion dollars in debt, but their personal assets stood at 64 trillion dollars. Others argue that we are sitting on a time-bomb.

Asset values will not continue to rise indefinitely and when they crash, millions of people will be plunged into negative equity. Liabilities remain the same but assets can go up and down in value. This was the case with stock market values, which saw sharp falls around 2000. Crisis was averted only because investors moved their money into real estate.

For millions of Americans this only confirmed the culture Alan Greenspan had been promoting – debt is good. And if he turns out to be wrong – well, we all had fun in the meantime.

5.2 Discussing costs *(page 52)*

CA = Cost accountant **GM** = General manager

CA Look, we've got to do something. Doing nothing is not an option. Our margins will just get squeezed more and more.

GM OK. What do you suggest?

CA Personally, I'd recommend cutting the wage bill – either by laying some people off or by freezing salaries.

GM Neither of which are going to be very popular options.

CA No, but the alternatives are probably worse: reducing material costs will definitely have an impact on product quality and cutting back on advertising expenditure is only a short-term solution – it will hurt us in the long run.

GM No, I see that. What about administrative costs or other overheads? Instead of cutting staff, we could try and do something about getting our energy bills down for example.

CA I've already done as much as I can in those areas. I have thought about this a lot and for me, the only real solution is to tackle labour costs. It may be painful, but the advantage of it would be that, once done, we could get back to concentrating on selling.

GM OK, I hear what you're saying, but I think it might create more problems than you think. I'm going to go away and think about it ... see if there is an acceptable way of doing it.

5.3 Exam spotlight, Key skill *(page 54)*

We are accused frequently of doing nothing about the ageing population and the consequent hole in pension funds. But you have to understand that, at the moment at any rate, there are no popular solutions to this problem. Either we raise the retirement age or we increase taxes on working people. Neither of these is a vote winner. I think a lot of us in government are hoping that if we just hold on a bit, then sooner or later another solution will present itself.

5.4 Exam spotlight, Exam practice *(page 55)*

1 I don't believe in the capital markets. For a start they are unpredictable and for another thing, not everyone has the possibility to take such risks with their money. I have always been of the view that you pay taxes through your working life in order to enjoy certain benefits from the state and certain protection against difficult times. For example, in case of unemployment or sickness or for your retirement, for that matter. So when I retire, I will live on what the government is due to give me. If I can't afford cruises in the Caribbean, then that's too bad.

2 I'm very lucky to have worked in the civil service, which has its own pension scheme. My salary has never been as good as it might have been in the private sector, but you accept that when you work for a public service. What you do get is job security, longer holidays, good medical insurance and an excellent pension. My pension is calculated as a percentage of my final salary. That's very rare in the private sector. Usually private companies take your average salary over a period of, say, twenty years. So all in all I expect to be very comfortable when I retire, even if I haven't had that much disposable income during my working life.

3 People think that as a company director, I'm bound to have all sorts of privileged pension benefits and company schemes going on – some special executive plan. But it's not the case. We have a company scheme for all our employees but I don't actually participate in it. Instead, I've put most of my money in a long-term savings account, that gives a good rate of return if you keep it in for long enough. It seems bizarre I know, but I make far more than I need to spend and I guess I'm naturally cautious with my money.

4 There's a saying – I don't know who by – that you should 'invest in land, because they don't make it any more!' I think that's good advice. Around 2004 there started to be a lot of stories in the media about company pensions and private pensions not delivering the benefits they had promised, mainly because they were linked to stock market investments. At that point I decided to withdraw my money from my own private pension and put it into property. I figured that if I bought a small office building, then by the time I reached retirement age, I would have paid off the mortgage and could live off the rent ... so that's what I did.

5 I realised quite early on that my state pension wasn't going to be sufficient, so I took out a private one when I was about 30. It works like a managed investment fund – a mixture of blue-chip stocks – so I don't really have much say in how the money is invested. Unfortunately, like a lot of private pension schemes, it hasn't really performed as predicted. I think the projected growth rate was between 8 and 12% and it's grown at about 4.5%, which isn't much above inflation. There are signs that the stock markets are doing a little better now, so I'm hopeful that in the long run I will have reasonable funds for my retirement. Would I advise anyone to do the same ... with hindsight, probably not.

Module 6

6.1 A contract to supply *(page 59)*

Barbara Paragon. Can I help you?

Paul Hello, is that Barbara?

Barbara Yes, speaking.

Paul Hi, Barbara, this is Paul from A1 Flooring in London. I'm just calling to discuss the extension of our contract for next year. Is this a good moment for you?

Barbara Yes, as good as any, I guess. Let me just get a pen and paper so I can make some notes ... OK, so where have we got to?

Paul Well, first the good news. The Klik laminate flooring has been going really well here – you'll probably have noticed that from the order book in the last six months or so. Customers really love it: the feedback we've had has been excellent.

Barbara That's great.

Paul It is good. I have to say, I'm not so surprised – it's an excellent product, very high quality and the price reflects that of course. Which brings me on to my next point. Now, I'm not asking for better commission – we're OK on that – but what would really help is more seasonal discounting from your end. What I mean is, reductions that we could pass straight on to our customers.

Generally, we run sales in January, spring and late summer and at the moment Paragon's products are the only ones that don't feature. I suppose you could say that gives them a certain exclusivity in the eyes of the customer, but at the same time ...

Barbara I can see the logic of what you're saying, and I've no doubt it would help sales, but what you must understand is that it's very difficult for us to have a policy with you that's different from all our other customers. Let me think ... what I could suggest is that we try and feed you more discounted stock when we are coming to the end of a particular product line. I can speak to the boss about that.

Paul Well, could you also mention to him the principle of seasonal discounts, because I think it would generate even more interest in the products.

Barbara All right, I will ... but I'm not too optimistic. Are there any other points?

Paul Yes, there is one other problem, which is that when we place an order, it's quite often the case that you don't have exactly what we want in stock and you offer us a substitute instead. Let me give you an example: we want engineered wood flooring in a natural oak and you only have it in a stained oak. On the whole we try to be flexible, but it's something which seems to be happening more and more – and that worries me.

Barbara I do understand, Paul, and I apologise. It's something which we are trying to solve. But it's not really a problem of our own making. It's a result of shortages in raw material and delays further up the supply chain. We do try to carry reserve stocks of all types of wood, but as you know it's a sensitive product to transport and store and we often have to rely on what's available from our suppliers at a given time. That's just the nature of the product.

Paul Yes, I appreciate all that, but explaining it to our customers is another thing. Often they're just not prepared to wait and if they can't get what they want exactly when they want it, they'll go elsewhere. In the end, that's no good for either of us. Are you saying that the situation is unlikely to improve because if you are ...

6.2 Telephone expressions *(page 62)*

Example

A Hello, is John there?
B Sure, I'll just get him for you.
A Thanks a lot.

1 A Can I speak to Yan Lin, please?
B I'm sorry, the line is engaged. Would you like to hold?
A No, that's OK. I'll call back later.

2 A I'm afraid Mr Chiu is out of the office today.
B OK. Can you take a message?
A Of course. I'll just get a pen and paper.

3 A Hello, Morris Industries.
B Can I have the sales department, please?
A One moment. I'll put you through.

4 A I'm afraid our computers are down at the moment.
B But I need the information by the end of today.
A OK, I'll get back to you as soon as I can.
B Thank you. I'd appreciate that.

5 A How can I help?
B Can you ask Esther to bring her laptop with her?
A Sure. I'll make sure she gets the message.
B Thanks.

6 A I'm calling about Mr Signelli. Is his bill for $3,000 or $3,500?
B One second. I'll just check my records.

7 A Can I speak to Sarah, please?
B Hang on. I'll see if she's back from lunch yet.

8 A So, it's the Taj Mahal restaurant at 1 o'clock.
B Great. I'll look forward to seeing you then.

Module 7

7.1 Strengths and weaknesses *(page 67)*

1 I admire my boss a lot. He's very capable; he knows exactly what he's doing and he's not afraid to get his hands dirty, not like some managers who think they're above it all. The one problem is that he takes on too much. I don't think it's because he doesn't trust us to do a good job – it's because he likes to be involved in everything. He's a bit of a control freak. The result is that he spreads himself very thin, when he could hand more work out to others, and he's often overloaded and stressed.

2 Cheryl's not particularly brilliant, but she knows that. She knows her own limitations, which is certainly one of her strengths. In fact, I don't think you have to be particularly bright to be a manager – that's more a quality you need in a leader. A manager's job is to bring order to the workplace and the team, so that people are clear about what they should be doing and when they should be doing it. Cheryl is very good at getting everyone working in the most efficient way and that makes our working environment much less stressful.

3 He's not an easy guy to work for. He has very high expectations of his staff and he can be rude and too direct. Sensitivity is not his strong point. He often puts you on the spot: 'What makes you think this will work?' 'Have you thought about the cost of this?' and so on. You have to be prepared to justify your actions a lot. Some people can't stand being challenged like this all the time, but you can't deny that he gets the most out of his staff. People do perform.

4 There are people who listen to what you are saying, and people who hear what you are saying. Paul is one of the former. He does try to listen to other people's ideas, but his mind has often moved onto the next thing, and he doesn't take on board what you're saying. It's the same thing when he's expressing his own ideas and wishes. He kind of takes it for granted that everyone has reached the same point in their thinking that he has, when often they're still two or three steps behind. Don't get me wrong, he's a very nice guy – kind and clever, and he has lots of great ideas and vision for the company – but because of these communication difficulties, he can be very frustrating to work for.

5 The financial rewards in our company are not so huge, but in spite of that, in my team we all stay very motivated because our boss really appreciates our work. She's actually very protective of her own people. She gives us a lot of praise. Other people in the company say she's a maverick, a kind of a loner. They say she's difficult to get on with and doesn't really have the company's interests at heart. But I wouldn't know about that really, because it's not the side of her that we see. What we get is 100% loyalty and encouragement.

Module 8

 8.1 Corporate social responsibility *(page 80)*

I'd like to talk to you today about an approach to doing business that is fast gaining popularity. It is the concept of Triple Bottom Line. We all know the term bottom line and what it refers to, namely the financial profitability of the company. Triple Bottom Line, or 3BL as it is sometimes called, recognises that there are two other important factors in measuring a company's success – social performance and environmental performance. Put in a more friendly way, 3BL is about 'People, Planet and Profits.' Nor are these things unconnected: the three legs are in fact strongly linked.

Why is this important? In today's global economy, the standards set by business, and not by government, are more and more what affect people's lives. The environment, as we all know, is under unprecedented pressure. In many sectors – transport, energy generation, production of chemicals and plastics – business can play its part in reducing pollution, particularly CO_2 emissions into the atmosphere. It can also take more responsibility for the full life-cycle of products – from manufacture to disposal.

In the area of social performance, businesses must consider the welfare of their employees and the communities in which they operate. In the pursuit of a better financial bottom line, companies will naturally look to reduce their labour costs. This may mean cutting jobs or wages or it may mean outsourcing work or relocating to a country where labour is cheaper. All too often the impact of these actions on the workforce is not taken properly into account.

One aspect of social responsibility – sponsorship of community projects – has already been taken up by companies on a wide scale. That is probably because companies have been quick to see the financial benefit of the good publicity that comes from being involved in such helpful projects.

Does all this sound nice? Of course it does, but it's not enough to say you are going to follow a policy of corporate social responsibility: to make a difference companies have to 'walk the talk.' So how do you go about translating good intentions into concrete actions that will really make a difference?

The first thing is to be attentive to the needs of all stakeholders. This means that companies must recognise their responsibilities not only to their shareholders, but also be committed to respecting their employees, their suppliers, their customers, and the local community and environment in which they operate.

The second point is about audits and reporting. Companies already submit their financial accounts for audit; they must also submit to social audits and environmental impact audits. These must be reported to the outside world so that everyone can see the results of their performance in the three key areas, thus tying companies to their promises. However, this means that companies have to be honest and open about their actions and so expose themselves to public criticism. It's easy to advertise your successes to your customer; it's not so easy to publicise the level of pollution from your factory or, if you are a private company, to disclose your financial results.

Module 9

 9.1 Market research *(page 86)*

Mr N = Mr Niedermeier **TM** = Telemarketer

Mr N Hello?

TM Sir, is that Mr Niedermeier?

Mr N Yes, it is. How can I help you?

TM Sir, I'm calling you from Arat Marketing. You're a holder of a gold Mastercard, is that correct?

Mr N Er ... yes, I am.

TM We are carrying out some market research on behalf of your bank. It's a short survey and to thank you for your time we would like to enter you for a prize draw to win an Aston Martin Vantage sports car. Would now be a convenient time or shall I call back later?

Mr N Umm ... how long will it take?

TM Only five minutes, sir.

Mr N And what is it for exactly? I'm not sure I understood.

TM It's a survey into consumer perceptions of brands. I'm going to give you the names of some well-known brands and I'd like you to give me one positive and one negative impression of this brand. If you don't have an impression say 'none.' If you have no knowledge of the brand say 'don't know.' Otherwise just keep your answers short and simple. Are you ready?

Mr N Er ... yeah, I guess so.

TM OK. Dell Computers. Have you ever bought one?

Mr N Yes.

TM One positive impression of the brand?

Mr N Umm ... good value for money.

TM And negative?

Mr N None.

 9.2 A product presentation *(page 87)*

Like most good innovations, the one I will present to you today is beautifully simple. Successful new products to my mind fall into two categories: firstly, those which are essentially luxuries. However seductively they're presented and packaged, they are unnecessary. And then there are those which are necessary, only people haven't realised it before because the product didn't exist. Which would you rather be selling? I know I'd rather be selling a neat solution to an unsolved problem.

OK, so, how many of you only remember to water your house plants when you see them wilting or dying? How many of you then spend the next month over-watering the plant until its roots start to rot and its leaves start to blacken? Come on, we've all done it.

Plant-carer is the answer to these problems. It's the brainchild of one of our R&D team, who made an early prototype of the product for his own use at home. Because he was on holiday for two weeks and had no-one in the block of apartments that he felt he could ask to look after his plants, he devised a simple automatic watering system. Basically, it consists of a container of water, a valve and a humidity sensor. When the humidity sensor detects that the earth in the plant pot is too dry, it causes a valve to open and release a fixed amount of water from the container into the plant pot. As long as the earth is damp, the valve remains closed.

We also have in the pipeline a more sophisticated model which can be used all the time, not just when you are away from home. With a range of settings, it allows you to set Plant-carer to deliver exactly the amount of water indicated in the plant care instructions, watering them as they need to be watered. The result is that the average person can care for a plant as an expert would.

I hope you're beginning to see the enormous potential we have here. This is a product that will appeal to everyone – not just limited to garden centres, or even DIY centres. Plant-carer is a product aimed at the mass market ... it can be sold also through every major supermarket in the country.

It comes in three sizes, the smallest retailing at an amazing €8. It complies with all health and safety regulations and doesn't need batteries or any other power source to run on.

I can't tell you how excited I am by the prospects for this product. It has the capability to transform this company; to do, even if it's on a smaller scale perhaps, what the Model T did for Ford and what the iPod did for Apple. Thank you.

9.3 Idioms *(page 90)*

M1 = Manager 1 **M2** = Manager 2

M1 As I see it, this is a job we can do – it's well within our capabilities. The only stumbling block is the price.

M2 I'll say. They're asking us to do something for a price which, quite frankly, for the work involved on our side, just isn't realistic!

M1 Yes, but you're assuming that we've got to start from scratch and that's not actually the case. It's not as pricey a job as you think. There's no need to reinvent the wheel, here. We can just take an existing piece of software and rework it.

M2 You say that, but I know what these projects are like. You imagine it's all going to be plain sailing, but then you inevitably run into one problem after another and before you know it, the costs have spiralled out of control.

M1 Of course there would be teething problems – there are with any project. And of course we would have to cost that in. But I'm sure we can find some middle ground with them.

M2 OK, but if it all goes pear-shaped, don't say I didn't warn you.

Module 10

10.1 A team-building day *(page 97)*

Well, hello. Good to see that you all made it – thank you. I hope that the programme I'm going to show you today will excite you as much as it does us. I should say before going through it, that although this will be a fun day, the ultimate aim is not just for everyone to have a good time, but to get to know each other better and to understand how each individual thinks, functions and likes to work. It's this understanding that will make us a stronger team.

I've written a summary of the programme on the handout you've all got in front of you and I'll just go through the schedule now. We'll meet here at 8am in the morning and be taken by coach direct to Silverstone racing circuit. That should take about 90 minutes. On arrival, we'll be met by Pauline Carter, who is our host for the day. She will explain the morning's activity and then we'll divide into four groups. Lunch will be at 1pm in the corporate hospitality suite in the main grandstand and we have a guest speaker lined up – his identity will remain a surprise for now. After lunch Pauline will take us back to the track for the afternoon's activities and we should be finished by about 4.30. We'll then have a debriefing session which will last about an hour. This is a chance for everyone to talk about their experiences of the day and should finish at about 5.30. The coach will bring us back to London by 7pm.

What will you be doing exactly? Well, I don't want to give away too much but I will tell you two things. First of all, you don't have to be a grand prix driver: that's to say, you won't have to drive a fast car if you don't want to. Secondly, there is much more to the tasks you will be undertaking than just driving skills and knowledge of motor sport.

So, how should you prepare? Please dress casually: jeans and training shoes (no high heels, please) and a jumper or warm jacket in case it's cold. You don't need to bring any of the following: money, mobile phones, PDAs, laptops. You can bring a camera if you want. Everything else you need will be supplied. As I said at the outset, I think it's going to be a really fun and exciting day and I hope it also achieves its aim of helping you to work more closely as a team. Now, are there any questions I can answer? Please remember that I can't really say more about the details of the event itself at the moment ...

10.2 Taking notes *(page 102)*

Hello David, Claudia – do have a seat. You're now coming towards the end of your training here – I hope you've both enjoyed your time. I've got one more task for you and this is it – please listen carefully. What I'd like you to do is to think about the office environment you've been working in for the last six months and to produce some proposals on how it could be improved.

There are some obvious areas to look at: because of the nature of our work and people being out of the office often, not everyone has his or her own desk and that can be a little frustrating. You may also think that the open plan office is a mistake – I certainly find it difficult sometimes when I have clients on the phone. Then there's the cosmetic side of it – people do comment on the décor being a little monotonous and impersonal – maybe that's just a matter of taste.

But these are conclusions I'd like you to draw for yourselves. I don't want to spoonfeed you or pre-empt your proposals. You've got a free hand, basically, and just three days. I suggest you spend the first couple looking around, talking to people, getting their views and write up your report on day three. One way or another I'd like the proposals on my desk first thing Thursday morning. Any questions?

Module 11

11.1 Relocation experiences *(page 111)*

1 A lot of regions try to attract companies by offering low business rates. That's why we originally moved here seven years ago. Unfortunately, it was just a carrot to get people like us to move here. It lasted for a while, but last year the local authority put up rates by a massive 30%. Now it's as expensive as anywhere else. If someone is thinking of moving for similar reasons, I'd advise against it. It's like sitting in the garden in the evening trying to stay in the sun – you keep moving your chair, but sooner or later the shade catches up with you.

2 We moved out here five years ago. Living in the city was expensive, but that wasn't the real motivation. I was commuting out to our offices every day, which are near the airport. It was taking me an hour and a half each way, which was crazy. Our house is now only ten minutes away, which is really handy – I can just take the bike or walk. It has other advantages too: the schools are great, there's lots of green space. Generally it's very peaceful, except when the planes go overhead: then you can't hear yourself think.

3 Competition is so tough in our field that reducing costs became a necessity. We didn't really want to move the operation, but in the end we had to get our wage bill under control. Moving to Hungary has been a great success: the people are highly skilled, hard-working and very productive. The salary bill is about half what it was, but it is creeping up. I guess that's inevitable with developing economies: people want more money to buy more expensive things.

4 We'd heard so many people say how stress-free life was in Australia, that we decided to take the plunge and move out here. And what they say is true: the people are relaxed, the sun shines and it's easy to get around. I say easy, but actually any trip becomes a major expedition. Australians will drive two hours to visit some friends without giving it a second thought. So we don't go out as much as we used to. When we do there are lots of things to do – it's not the cultural desert that people in Europe make out it is.

5 Basically, it was just a lack of space. Our business was growing and we couldn't keep the level of stock that the orders demanded. We've now got more than enough – I just hope business stays buoyant. It has made delivery a little more expensive because we're not as central as we were – most of our customers are in the London area. But you can't have it both ways. On the other hand, our suppliers probably find it easier to get stock to us, so I suppose the move has benefited them.

Module 12

 12.1 Understanding business culture *(page 121)*

John So, Jim, what did you know about doing business in China before you made your first trip there?

Jim Very little, actually. These days there's a lot of literature and advice out there. I had heard about the principle of Guanxi before I went to China, but I hadn't really realised how important a part of business culture it was.

John What is Guanxi, exactly?

Jim It refers to relationships or connections with people that are built on trust and have been developed over a long time. These relationships are based on shared experience – people operating in a similar field – and often also on the exchange of gifts or favours.

John But if you're an outsider, that must make life very difficult. You don't have a shared background as such ...

Jim That's right. You don't have those networks and for that reason you're going to have to be patient, because it takes time to develop them. That's why so many foreign businesses look for a Chinese partner who has good contacts already, like an agent or business partner.

John And is there any other way to shortcut this process?

Jim Not really. Gift-giving is helpful – presenting a small gift at the end of a meeting, for example. Don't expect immediate returns, though, and don't give anything big. The Chinese government has clamped down hard on bribery in recent years and won't tolerate it. What you have to do is build friendships.

John And how would you go about that? Any particular tips?

Jim There's no particular secret: just get to know your partners, exchange small talk, invite them out for meals – Chinese people love eating out. They'll certainly invite you out to a restaurant at some point. The main thing is just to be yourself ... with an extra bit of formality and politeness. Don't do what some people do and try to be Chinese.

John And are there any things you shouldn't talk about – any taboos?

Jim Umm ... I think the important thing is to show genuine interest in learning about China and its customs, and to be respectful of the country and the government. There are also a few different habits. Sometime during the meal there will be toasts – make sure that you make one to the most senior member of the group there.

John Any other tips?

Jim Well, they appreciate the best – established brands with a quality reputation – having had limited access to western products in the past. Everyday practicalities? Er ... people dress soberly for business, they shake hands on meeting ... usually, though occasionally they'll just nod at you. They love to exchange business cards, so bring lots of those. And when you receive one make sure you study it carefully – it's very rude just to put it straight in your pocket.

John What about their behaviour? The Chinese have a reputation for being difficult to read.

Jim I don't really find that. Perhaps they use facial expressions or gestures less freely than westerners do. They do seem to take their time agreeing to things. There are two reasons for that: first of all, they generally operate within big hierarchies and the decision may need to come from high up; secondly, they dislike saying 'no' directly. If they start to make a series of small objections to something, it generally means they're trying to say they're not interested. But above all, as I said before, don't worry about the time all this takes – you're going to need that anyway to learn how Chinese companies operate and all the governance and tax laws, the regulations around joint ventures and so on ...

12.2 Small talk: short responses *(page 122)*

Sarah Hi, Joachim, sorry to be a little late.

Joachim No problem. Good to see you again. How was your trip?

Sarah It was fine. No delays, just the usual traffic from the airport.

Joachim And did you find our offices easily?

Sarah Yes, thank you. Your directions were very clear.

Joachim OK. So, can I get you a coffee before we start?

Sarah Yes. I'd love one. White, one sugar, please.

Joachim And, how are you fixed for time?

Sarah I've got a couple of hours now. I hope that's enough.

Joachim Sorry, do you mind if I just take this call?

Sarah No, of course not. Go ahead ...

Joachim Sorry about that – the boss. So, are you expecting it to be a good year?

Sarah Well, I hope so. Last year was pretty flat, as you know.

Joachim Well, that's really what I'd like to talk about today – how we can ramp things up a bit. Can I be of any help with the marketing side of things?

Sarah That's kind of you, but we should be able to cope. It's just a question of programming it in. We're planning a campaign meeting next week ...

Joachim ... so I think that's been a useful start to our discussions. I will programme another meeting for two weeks' time. But I think you have to go now. Would you like to go for a meal this evening?

Sarah I'd love to, but I'm afraid I have to be back in London by six.

Joachim No worries. Would you like a lift back to the station?

Sarah That would be really nice, but I don't want to put you out.

Joachim It's no problem. I'm going that way anyway.